THE LIMELIGHT

THE LIMELIGHT

A Compendium of Contemporary Columbia Artists

Volume III

Edited by
Cynthia Boiter

THE LIMELIGHT: A COMPENDIUM OF CONTEMPORARY COLUMBIA ARTISTS, VOLUME III

Copyright 2022 by Cynthia Boiter. All rights reserved. Printed in Columbia, SC in the United States of America. No part of this book may be used or reproduced without written permission from the publisher except in the case of brief quotations embodied in critical articles and reviews. For further information address Muddy Ford Press, 1009 Muddy Ford Road, Chapin, South Carolina 29036.

www.MuddyFordPress.com

Library of Congress Number: 2022951103

ISBN: 9781942081326

Cover Art by Michael Krajewski

Terry—played by Claire Bloom: "I thought you hated the theatre?"

Calvero—played by Charlie Chaplin: "I also hate the sight of blood, but it's in my veins."

>From the film The Limelight, 1952

Created when an oxyhydrogen flame is directed at a cylinder of calcium oxide, known as quicklime, the limelight was first used in London's Covent Garden Theatre in 1837 to illuminate the stars of the stage.

Table of Contents

Preface – *Cindi Boiter* — 1

Tom Beard – *Jon Tuttle and Josh Tuttle* — 3

Al Black – *Cassie Premo Steele* — 9

Nappy Brown – *Clair DeLune* — 17

Anastasia Chernoff – *Cindi Boiter* — 23

Thorne Compton – *Dale Bailes* — 35

Clark Ellefson – *Kristine Hartvigsen* — 39

William Price Fox – *David Axe* — 49

Phillip Gardner – *Jon Tuttle* — 53

Tyrone Geter – *Claudia Smith Brinson* — 61

Terrance Henderson – *Jason Stokes* — 69

Rob Kennedy – *Ed Madden* — 75

Jillian Owens – *Cindi Boiter* — 89

Leslie Pierce – *Ed Madden* — 93

Kathleen Robbins – *Tim Conroy* — 95

Sharon Strange – *Len Lawson* — 103

Kay Thigpen – *Chad Henderson* — 117

Preface

More time has passed than I intended between the release of the second volume of the *Limelight: A Compendium of South Carolina Artists* and this third volume you hold in your hands. The second volume was timely, just two years following the first. We were doing well.

It would be easy to argue that the momentum has been lost. Some of the essays contained herein have a bit of dust on them. Some may be a little wrinkled around the edges.

There's an explanation.

To say that much has happened over the past seven years since we celebrated the birth of the last Limelight volume is like taking the first breath with which you'll tell the story of your life. There are few good metaphors to describe what happens to a culture after it sustains the injuries of a global pandemic, more than four years of a potential despot and consequent imperiled democracy, the long-awaited response to so much social injustice that the only place to be heard is from the street, and war abroad with the sour smelling reminder that war at home is not impossible at all.

Some of us survived. Sadly, some of us did not.

This volume of *The Limelight* is not as joyous as were the first two. More time has passed. More of our colleagues have left us and you'll read about them in these pages. Anastasia, Leslie, Jillian, Kay, Thorne, Nappy Brown, and more. Their stories are their legacies and it's so easy now to see the places where the streams and rivulets of the energy they expended on earth stretched and meandered.

How many of us sat in the theatre that Kay Thigpen created with her husband Jim and felt windows opened and walls blown down in our souls and psyches by what was given to us from her stage?

How wide is the tribal circle that Anastasia Chernoff created when she invited us all, everyone who would come, to her expansive cave of creative genius?

How many hearts and heads will Thorne Compton continue to teach and touch as the currents of his influence forever surge through the culture he helped create?

The only way to quelch the pain of losing icons like these is to celebrate them and see their work, the patterns they established, the inspiration they shared, in the lives and work of the artists whose work is still part of our everyday lives. Kathleen, Al, Terrance, Clark, and so many more included in these pages as well as those about which we've yet to write.

As we read these pages let's commit ourselves to taking notice of the artists in our lives and in our neighborhoods and determine whose stories we will preserve for posterity in the next volume of *The Limelight*. Who will we write about while they read their stories themselves? Let me know and I promise to put those pages in your hands sooner rather than later. No one has time to waste.

Cindi Boiter
March 2022

Tom Beard —
Fanfare for an Uncommon Man

By Josh Tuttle and Jon Tuttle

Part I: Toccata: a short composition demonstrating technical expertise

Our server at Lula Drake is discovered lingering nearby, eavesdropping on our conversation. "I'm sorry," she says. "I can't help it. This is so interesting."

For an hour or so we've been sitting with Tom Beard, discussing the influence of 19th century science and philosophy on art and culture, as one would. Also, seafood. Also, family. Also, everything in the world, known and unknown. And, at one point, the role of musical director, of which he is the Midlands' preeminent.

Since 1989, Tom has served as musical director on more than thirty productions, most recently for *The Restoration's Constance* at Trustus, a gorgeous, sprawling epic set in reconstruction-era Lexington: before that, some of the classics of American musical theatre, including *next to normal, Spring Awakening, Sweeney Todd, Hedwig and the Angry Inch, Kiss of the Spider Woman, Into the Woods* and *Big River*. As musical director, he is conductor, performer, composer, and arranger, customizing and interpreting the parts to fit the number and skillsets of his performers and improvising changes in orchestration. He's also a sound designer. And an actor. And the guy in a Trustus production of *Passing Strange* who stopped conducting and yelled, "What about The Clash, man?"

And he's ubiquitous as a keyboardist in, for instance, a jazz duo at Nonnah's in the Vista, in Opera USC's *Sunday in the Park With*

George, in Theatre Raleigh's production of *Master Class*, and at the Columbia Museum of Art, or as an accompanist for MFA vocal performance students at USC, or at Southeastern Theater Conference auditions.

No wonder his command of all spheres of musicology go is expansive. He moves lithely from a Schenkerian analysis of Bach and its correlation with John Coltrane's harmonic language to retrograde figures in the serialist music of Schoenberg, and then to the Beatles, about whom he taught a course at USC, and then to Rainer Maria Rilke, who once wrote, in a letter to a younger poet:

> *Being an artist means not reckoning and counting but ripening like the tree that stands confident in the storms of spring without fear that after them may come no summer. It does come. But it comes only to the patient, who are there as though eternity lay before them. I learn it daily, learning with pain for which I am grateful. Patience is everything.*

"Ah Rilke," Tom will observe later. "I haven't read him in such a long time, but I love his organic metaphor of ripening, and he was definitely a counter-voice to all those acidic Austrian fin-de-siècle musicians, writers, painters and philosophers who I couldn't read enough of."

And so on, into the afternoon, Tom leaning into the conversation, nodding, affirming, connecting, while the server hovers nearby. Laughter. Emphasis. Revelation. Until one is reminded of Jennie Jerome, Winston Churchill's mother, who had occasion to dine with William Gladstone and, several nights later, Benjamin Disraeli. When asked her impressions, she is said to have said: "When I left the dining room after sitting next to Gladstone, I thought he was the cleverest person in England. But when I sat next to Disraeli, I left feeling that I was."

Part II: Fugue: a contrapuntal composition in which a short phrase is

introduced and successively interwoven with others

> *"I live my life in widening circles that reach out across the world."*
> *– Rilke*

"He always makes you feel like you are the most important person in the room."
–Becky Hunter

"In my imagination, when I am with Tom we are singing, powerfully, melodically, joyfully, and that music fills my heart."
–Thorne Compton

"He's such a stickler when it comes to precise musicianship that it makes you feel incredible after learning something new from him."
–Avery Bateman

"In my dreams, when I'm singing, Tom is playing. His integrity is his charm. An improvisational genius overflowing with generosity of spirit and kindness of heart. A beautiful, free minded, loving human being who sees the world in color. A man whose hands and heart are synonymous with music."
–Terrance Henderson

> *"Let everything happen to you. Beauty and terror: just keep going. No feeling is final."*
> *–Rilke*

"He will hold your hand through the scary parts and catapult you to things you never thought you could do."
–Mindi Penn

"The thing I value most is his faith in my abilities. One of my favorite memories: I was looking at a piece of music from the show I was auditioning for, convinced I could never hit the high note. Tom finally smiled and—waving his hands a bit and tucking his hair behind his ears—said, 'You can hit it, believe me. Just stop *looking* at the notes and *sing* them.'"
–Kim Harne

"He taught me: no judgement. He cares, always."
–Steve Harley

> *"Describe your sorrows and desires, the thoughts that pass through your mind and your belief in some kind of beauty–describe all these with heartfelt, silent, humble sincerity and, when you express yourself, use the Things around you, the images from your dreams, and the objects that you remember."*
> *–Rilke*

"Tom knew of my great fondness for *Gilligan's Island*, and every night of Workshop's *Young Frankenstein* he would subtly insert the opening fanfare of the theme song into one of my songs."
–Frank Thompson

"I love that he adds flourishes during performances to keep himself from getting bored; scores are too tethering for his genius."
–Patrick Kelly

"He *is* music."
–Mary Jeffcoat

Part III: Rhapsody: an instrumental composition creating effusive or ecstatic feeling

She reappears. "Would you like some more wine?"

We would.

What were we talking about? Oh yes: the long arc of experience, how life, as Tom Stoppard described the art of adaptation, is not to be lived by proceeding from point-to-point in some premeditated fashion, but by spotting a hilltop in the faraway distance and aiming toward it. Improvising. Changing. Trusting.

Patience is everything.

Tom writes later: "My life has been such a patchwork-in-progress, and it is only now that I start to see more clearly how much there is I'd like to do and create. I often feel that until now it's been a long vaudeville act of keeping six dishes spinning on wooden sticks while riding my unicycle and whistling snatches of Sondheim."

We learn that for over twenty years he's worked as a Computer Programmer or Applications Analyst or Database Administrator for various South Carolina agencies, including USC: not the sort of career you'd imagine for someone whose professional life began when he was a teenager playing piano on a riverboat at Carowinds. Not the sort of career you'd imagine for a self-described "unruly goof" who'd entertain his classmates with ventriloquist and magic shows; who was president of his drama club; who, in "You're a Good Man, Charlie Brown," played Snoopy alongside Leeza Gibbons' Peppermint Patty.

More plausible by far that he would be a theater major, which he was, at USC, but only long enough to meet Carol Pabst in Ann Dreher's Children's Theatre class. By the time they married, in 1980, he'd finished his baccalaureate degree, *cum laude,* in Philosophy, and would soon earn a master's.

He explains: "I found philosophy a mindfully foundational approach to the world, and the history of philosophy a profound study of the source of Western intellectual and cultural history. It helps us simply stop and be patient without panting for definitive answers, and discuss those recurring questions which, though unanswerable, are still inescapable. 'What is justice?' 'How do you know what you think you know?' 'What do we owe each other?'"

> *"Be patient toward all that is unsolved in your heart and try to love the questions themselves."*
> *–Rilke*

Mention is made of Morse Peckham, a mentor at USC who opened his home and his mind to students like Tom for whom enough was never enough.

Mention is made of a book popular in the 1980's, Douglas Hofstadter's *Godel Escher Bach*, which uses math, art and music to show how cognition is formed and systems of thought create meaning. "What's even more exciting," Tom writes later, "is the ever-growing confirmation by scientific evidence of many of the observational psychological data discussed in the East for 2500 years—the achievements in understanding neuroplasticity and attention-focus training to re-wire the neural networks of our brains."

And later: "to me all great art is intrinsically pluralistic—it marinates in diversity and laughs at accusations of contradiction. This is what gives art its power and of endless growth."

And now she is back. Perhaps she never left. "Have you had enough?" she asks.

No. We have not.

Al Black
Branches of the Same Tree

By Cassie Premo Steele

> "If what I say resonates with you, it's merely because we're branches of the same tree."
> –W.B. Yeats

This difference is very noticeable

An out-of-state poet and editor of an online journal was reading in town. As the mother of a young child, I never made it out to the big poetry venue that started late at the Art Bar, but this one was different. It started earlier. And was at a place that served vegan food, which meant that I could also get myself a good dinner. Win-win for a poet-mom. So, I went.

And in addition to a beautiful poetry reading, I received the gift of meeting Al Black for the first time.

Booming northern accent, warm handshake, and a welcoming presence for a diverse audience – this difference is very noticeable, I thought to myself.

Columbia would never be the same.

Neither would I.

Stir it up

When we try to trace the origin of something, the roots are often hidden, and we have to be content with counting branches.

Al Black's branches reach out across the city in unexpected ways. But the strongest branch has always been Mind Gravy Poetry, a weekly event that Al leads featuring a poet and a musician and an open mic. That first venue on North Main gave way to others—a coffee shop in Five Points, a Mexican restaurant in the Vista, a pizza place in Rosewood, and more.

The diversity of the venues parallels the diversity of the featured performers and the audience. I noticed this the first time I attended.

As Al said, "I looked around and I either saw academic events, black events or white events.... I'm about unity, so I purposely started Mind Gravy with the design and the desire to stir it up."

He isn't exaggerating about the segregation in this city.

I was meeting an artist in town one day, and I told her I was going to pick up my middle-school aged stepdaughter at basketball practice at a nearby park. She told me she'd never heard of that park.

It was less than a mile from her house.

It was a "black" park.

This conversation took place before Al Black moved here.

It was before he started running his weekly Mind Gravy Poetry, as well as the three monthly events he also leads: Songversations, Bones of the Spirit, and Magnify Magnolias.

If things have gotten better in this city -- more inclusive, less segregationist, less university-centered, more accepting of difference – it's mostly because of Al Black.

I'm not exaggerating when I say this.

I have coffee with friends

Alice Walker says that writers should make time and space for writing "as if you were going to have someone come to tea."

Al Black does just this. But he does it by having coffee with friends.

In addition to running four regular poetry and music events in the city, Al has also published two full books of poetry and co-edited the volume, *Hand to Hand: Poets Respond to Race* with poet Len Lawson, as well as doing hundreds of poetry readings and writing thousands of poems.

How does he do it?

Columbia being a southern city, the friends are often late meeting him at the coffee shop. So, he writes then.

Because poetry does not come in the early or late times, but only always now.

Or his conversation over coffee with a friend meanders into unforeseen territories of memory and emotion.

So, he stays at the table after the friend leaves and writes then. Because poetry will always come when welcomed.

Or someone invites him over for root beer.

As I did.

And he will say yes.

Because poetry always says yes.

No turning back

"Is she here?" he asked.

"Soon," I said. "She's on her way from work."

Al hesitated in the doorway.

"I..." he started, "I have a policy that I don't meet a woman alone in a home."

I nodded.

We both loved Anne Sexton's poetry and shared enough of her story to know that this policy probably came from a history that was better left unspoken and even better honored.

"How about sitting on the porch then?" I smiled. "Would that work?"

We settled on the porch with root beer and did small talk until she arrived.

And then we told him.

We had fallen in love, we said, and we had told our husbands.

No one else in town knew.

Al was the one person we trusted with the news.

We talked for hours. I brought out cookies. He ate them all. I brought another root beer. He drank it. The sun went down. We were still on the porch. He had to meet his wife Carol for dinner, he said.

We thanked him for his visit.

It was not what we meant to say.

What we meant to say was "Thank you for being the father we needed at this moment, someone to listen and nod your head and understand what we are saying and see on our faces what we are feeling and give us perspective from your years of fathering and warn us of the hardship that is coming and encourage our love that is blossoming and call us your daughters of light."

We didn't say this.

He knew what we meant, though.

And years later, he would sing at our wedding.

Only concentric circles

If every word is potentially a poem and every branch can give birth to a seed for the next tree, then it's not only impossible to trace the origins of something but also its growth in the coming generations.

Time and meaning are slippery.

And yet, what poets do — what Al does — is to grab hold tight and say, "This matters."

Diversity in a southern city matters. Poetry and music matter. Conversations matter. Independent coffee shops matter. Black lives matter. Families and friendships matter. Love matters.

I knew all this about Al as the leader in our community.

But I learned something else about him when he became my student in the monthly Earth Joy Writing workshops I led at Saluda Shoals Park for over a year.

I learned that despite all the talk and northern bravado and history of jockness and genius coaching and successful businessman and tireless organizer and unconditional encourager of artists, there is a boy.

There is a boy riding his bike in Indiana. There is a boy walking in the woods. There is a boy catching fireflies. There is a boy wanting to be good.

It is this boy who, daily, creates the good man that Al Black is.

If more men were like Al and could be boys daily, instead of being content with the jagged edges where stories of success and collective violence meet, imagine the concentric circles that this could create. Imagine the world this would be.

The old tree fell over

And yet, even concentric circles come to the edge of the pond, and the Great Lakes and the Atlantic Ocean have shores. Without these shores, where would we live?

Everything ends.

We are here now.

It is the deep understanding of this that makes an artist.

I said before that one secret to Al's poetry success is coffee. The other secret is that he hardly sleeps.

Often, he is awake late into the night, writing. I get up early. So early that for many people, it is still night. But for me, it is pre-dawn. It is the confluence of light and dark, in the world and in us, in Al and me, that is, I believe, what makes us poets and what forges our connection.

One morning, for example, after finishing my writing, I checked Facebook and discovered that Al had posted the quote from Yeats that opens this essay only hours before.

And around the same time, I was writing a poem in my journal that ends with "shadows and fear are illusions in this place of tree and fire, wood and flame, here."

Al will be wood one day. I will, too.

This isn't maudlin, as some of our biological family members would have us believe. It is what makes us who we are, as poets, as teachers, as leaders, as father and daughter.

All old trees fall over. Some young ones do.

We don't know when. Or what will happen then. But as Al writes,

> it is enough
> to know
> that you are here,
> that you have today,
> that this is all
> you've been asked
> to handle
> and that is OK.

Notes

"This difference is very noticeable" is from "Winter Poem" in *I Only Left for Tea*: Poems by Al Black (Muddy Ford Press, 2014), page 71.

"Stir it up" is from "Local Poet and Arts Advocate Al Black Works Tirelessly to Open Opportunities for Diverse Artists" by Rodney Welch in *Free Times*, September 28, 2016.

"I have coffee with friends" is from "When I Was Nine" in I Only Left for Tea, page 26.

"as if you were going to have someone come to tea" is from "Alice Walker Offers Advice on Writing" by Jessica Strawser, August 31, 2010.

"no turning back" is from "Daughter of Light" in *I Only Left for Tea*, page 42.

"Only concentric circles" is from "Leaping fish" in *The Man with Two Shadows* by Al Black (Muddy Ford Press, 2018), page 38.

"the old tree fell over" is from "Firewood" " in *The Man with Two Shadows*, page 59.

"it is enough…" is from "Enough" in *The Man with Two Shadows*, page 58.

Nappy Brown
Wistful Remembrances of Nappy's Giving Spirit

By Clair DeLune

When humans are faced with a novel and difficult challenge, history shows that — as a whole — we rise above and meet the challenge head on to beat it. But few talk about the preparation, and sometimes hesitation, we must overcome to do so.

Part of that process involves looking back on "old times" with a wistful spirit. That can either inspire positive feelings or it can bring one down. The difference is in whether or not one can find the hope and look forward to better times ahead, which often depends upon the role models who have taught us fortitude, endurance and to have faith in ourselves and the goodness of others.

Long before the recent worldwide pandemic turned our lives inside out, I was given the honor of writing about my dear friend, Nappy Brown, from an artist-to-artist perspective.

I developed a deep friendship with this talented Blues Shouter via my work in music history, specifically teaching Blues and Rock & Roll History at the University of South Carolina, as well as through producing and hosting a complementary radio show on WUSC-FM to air the music to my classes and the public.

Nappy, who originally shot to fame in the 1950s along with the likes of Little Richard, Big Maybelle, Jimmy Reed and Big Mama Thornton, was a frequent guest performer in class and on the radio – reticent at first, but as we got to know each other through the years, he opened up and his big heart became evident through his stories, trademark thousand-watt smile and a sometimes mischievous glint in his eyes as he would confide a story with a plea to never repeat it as he told it over the air; adding a conspiratorial wink.

His goodness, as well as that of his wife of 30 plus years – Miss Cora – who is the human equivalent of a warm hug, was revealed through the years as I enjoyed many get-togethers with them at their church, their home and at performances.

Each year, their tiny white wooden church would host an anniversary gospel fest to celebrate the date that Nappy Brown joined *The Faithful Workers* choir.

I often drove up with friends to enjoy the preaching, gospel music and fellowship at Nappy and Cora's little chapel located near Newberry, S.C. Some years, I attended with my entire class of music appreciation students – many of whom still count it as one of the most moving experiences of their lives, even so long afterwards.

The weather is often hot and muggy during early summer in South Carolina. The air is thick with humidity, and the insect choruses hidden within the deeply forested woodlands outside the country chapel would make themselves known long before the choirs arrived.

And arrive they did.

An endless array of soloists, duos, trios, quartets, quintets and full choirs would pull up in buses and automobiles to emerge in long, colorful robes or shiny silk dresses and suits. The event began at 5 p.m., and the varied and sundry church fans batting away heat and the occasional insect looking for a meal stopped flapping, and heads turned to the back of the church when Nappy's deeply compelling voice would call out to God and all others in earshot, "Down in the Valley," as the Faithful Workers slowly stepped their awesome processional up the aisle.

This Episcopalian had always wanted to attend a gospel service, but nothing could have prepared me for the exuberance of the first celebration I experienced. Clapping and "Amen" and "Hallelujah" and shouts of joy emanated – not only from the choir, but from the parishioners – differing from quiet, subdued "Catholic Lite" services I'd grown up with. As a child, I thought one particular soloist had sung beautifully, so I clapped, but my circumspectly sweet Mother kindly corrected my "outburst of appreciation" by placing her white-gloved hand atop my overly clap-happy ones.

Nary was a soul left out that day in the countryside of South Carolina - righteous expressions of the spirit of glory lifted the roof off that tiny house of worship. With the freely appreciative glory of being able to clap and sing along with the gospel spirit flowing through us all, I decided I had found a home in that sanctuary.

Here's what I did not know: once again, because of my upbringing in a church where the service starts on time, and heaven forbid the sermon were to go on more than 15 minutes, and you get a processional with robes and incense and kneel every two minutes to pray (keeping knee replacement surgeons in business, I suspect); then two more hymns, perhaps communion, then boom – out by noon to race to be first at local restaurants...

...what I did not know was that Nappy's jubilee was not a 5-6 p.m. event. It went on until nearly 11 p.m. without a break. Groups drove from all over the Southeast to sing one song apiece in tribute to Nappy, then left for the long drive back in the deep darkness along two-lane, winding, country roads.

One song each. And it took six hours. Do the math.

That was one hell of a church tribute, if you will pardon my rule breaking. I figure if you can clap in church now, the word hell must be okay, too. Besides, it is in the Bible – so St. Peter cannot get too mad at me. If he is, I'll have to make it up before judgment day, right?

One of my companions reminded me recently that Nappy surprised me at my first attendance by asking me to come up to the apse of the chapel to "say a few words." No warning. No prep. And I was dumbstruck and confounded as to what on earth I had to contribute in words. I do remember the feeling of stage fright as I stood, wondering what to say, but I'm told I shared much of what I'm about to relate to you next.

The warmth of Nappy and Cora is in their giving spirit. The endless stream of tributes from gospel groups is one measure. And Nappy has given the clothes off his back to others in need – notably Chuck Berry, with whom he shared a show on a date when Chuck's wardrobe failed to arrive. Nappy told Chuck he could pick a suit of clothes out of his wardrobe. Nappy laughed loudly, "He took my gold *lamé* suit – my best one! And I never got it back!"

We all know the one.

Little Richard's death in May of 2020 brought memories back of seeing Little Richard play at the South Carolina State Fair in 1998, toward the end of his performing days. Out of everyone in the grandstand, he spied Nappy Brown, dressed very casually, and screamed in his inimitable voice, "Nappy Brown! Is that YOU? You come right on up on stage here with me," to which Nappy bowed and shook his head. Little Richard insisted; so up Nappy went to perform an unrehearsed duet with his longtime friend. Little Richard hugged him closely; laid his head on Nappy's shoulder, then proudly announced, "This man helped make me who I am."

Nappy would be invited on stage everywhere he went by giants like Little Richard, Buddy Guy and Screamin' Jay Hawkins, to name a few. Nappy would grace the stage with them; his bigger-than-life persona and voice rising up, whether amplified or not.

His grace and spirit never gave the sense that he might have been a bigger, more famous artist than those who extolled his influence on their work and style. He was a giver, not a taker. He loved his life at home with Cora and the family; but at times, sitting in the back den with him, he'd proudly say how much he enjoyed his tours, extolling his fans in foreign countries and mentioning he "really loved that *sake* in Japan," where neither the Blues and R&B, nor Nappy himself, ever went out of style.

One could not fail to note when entering their modest home that the size of the pots on the stove is only exceeded by the size of their hearts. They would feed everyone. Food for the soul, hence "Soul Food." We in South Cackalacky just call it country cooking. Fried chicken, mashed potatoes, collards with ham hocks, corn on the cob, sweet taters and endless other dishes fed the body after we would return from an enormous drink from the spiritual fountain that filled our souls.

Long after Nappy's death, I still stay in touch with Miss Cora and love to hear her deep Southern accent call out "How ah you, Clah-rah?" She and I worked diligently together in 2014 on the chapter of my book, South Carolina Blues, which featured Nappy. Her generosity with time and stories was only exceeded by her patience in entrusting me with three family albums of photos of Nappy and Cora's family and friends. I will always be grateful she trusted me so completely during that year it took me to digitize them before returning those precious artifacts to their rightful place.

The gift of those memories and the example of people who care more about giving to others is uplifting and makes it possible to look forward to the likelihood of having warm gatherings at some point in the future with loved ones whom we miss now.

That is the gift that keeps giving from the blessing of having had Nappy and Cora as my dear friends for so many wonderful years.

These COVID19 days might be times to be "gotten through," but sometimes the best memories are made or emerge from hardships.

The lessons they teach us about the greater good that is possible are treasures.

Even apart – we are bound together by music, faith, love, and wonderful memories.

Anastasia Chernoff
So Much Love To Be Gone So Soon

By Cindi Boiter

I first met Anastasia on the sidewalk of Main Street in Columbia, SC. She was coming out of a space that was showing art with a large-for-Columbia entourage, and I was going in.

This was during Anastasia's hat phase. For a while, she wore hats everywhere she went, weather be damned. Cowboy hats. Fedoras. Tams and berets. It was about the hat, to some degree. But it was also about her, to be honest, whether she realized it or not.

It was about the statement she wanted to make to the world that we shouldn't mistake her for a normal woman. An average person. A mere mortal.

It was a signal.

In was, with great humility, a nod to the world that she had accessed what was special about herself, operationalized it, engaged it, empowered it, and launched it full force onto life's stage. No apologies and no holding back.

But, even more than that, especially more than that, it was her tip of the hat to the people she encountered letting them know that she expected no less from us, either. And she didn't stop there. If we didn't already know what was special about us, Anastasia would help us find it.

And once our specialness, the thing about ourselves that made us unique—the gifts we could give that no one else could give like we could—was discovered, she would make it sacred.

I still carry the part of myself that Anastasia made sacred inside of me. And I'm not the only one in Columbia, South Carolina who does so.

I had been hearing about Anastasia for a while before I met her. The beautiful and much younger wife of Marvin Chernoff.

This was just before she opened her gallery in the front of the Free Times space on Main Street, when Main Street Columbia was in the process of becoming a hub for artists and arts lovers. Paintings were going up on empty walls and makeshift stages were being assembled of plywood and concrete blocks in roped off parking spaces. The crowds hadn't quite reached critical mass yet. We were still a little outlaw—asking for forgiveness rather than permission, and very much aware that we were on the verge of something exciting.

When the group of friends with whom I was walking intersected the group of friends with whom Anastasia was walking, we stopped abruptly and a second or two passed before Anastasia crossed the circle and enveloped me in a full-body embrace. The kind that you hold a little too long, but your bodies are rocking side-to-side together and it feels too good to stop.

I knew that I knew of Anastasia, but I had no idea that she knew of me.

"Cindi!" she called out like I was her long-lost sister and she had been on a quest to rescue me from foul weather or imminent danger.

When her hug was over, she began to touch my face and rub my upper arms with the comforting caress of a mom or a grandmother and coo some throaty language at me that wafted through my senses on little multi-hued, effervescent clouds of patchouli. I instantly felt seen. And loved.

It was one of those times when I self-consciously, but still truly, wondered if I knew someone from another life.

Marvin met Anastasia in her floral shop in 2000 and, even though he had more than twice her 31 years under his belt, the two fell in love and married within a year. Actually, it was probably because of Marvin's advanced age that their romance moved so intensely and quickly. As those of us who have reached a certain age know, Marvin must have known not to waste a moment of time being without the beautiful and magical Anastasia in his life.

People with boring lives gossiped about their May-December relationship. People who knew Anastasia simple thought, *smart man*.

Though other men came into Anastasia's life once Marvin transitioned into the role of her "wasband," as she called him, he remained a part of her most immediate family and tribe, often sharing long and glorious meals in the little house he restored for her on Park Street with some of her other loves. Anastasia's beliefs about love and intimacy could not be constrained by archaic cultural constructs that limited the full and expansive expression of her emotions.

Anastasia's artistic journey wasn't paved with the sunshine and daffodils the artist's exceedingly pleasant personality suggested. But it may be the hardships she underwent that led her to the place of prominence she held on Columbia's social scape, and the priority she placed on treating people as kindly as she wanted to be treated herself.

The daughter of Ann Smith Hankins, a single parent who escaped from a bad marriage with her baby and a huge tub of crayons in tow, Anastasia lived alone with her mother from the time she was a toddler until Hankins remarried when Anastasia was nineteen.

"My mom was a good role model for me in terms of teaching me how to be independent," Anastasia told me when I interviewed her for an article in the fourth issue of *Jasper Magazine*. And despite the fact that she almost constantly surrounded herself with people she loved, Anastasia's independence of spirit was reflected nowhere more than in the art she created as a sculptor.

Anastasia could trace her love of the malleability of clay back to her earliest days of childhood when her grandmother would give her a spoon and a plastic container to play with in the dirt at her West Columbia home. "I would come home from school and stay with my grandmother and grandfather while my mom worked," she said. "Being able to play outside in the dirt and clay at my grandmother's was like heaven to me."

Born to a mother who was only 17 years old, Anastasia didn't talk much about her father, though she had memories of him cropping up throughout her childhood. Anastasia, who valued empathy and compassion in herself and others, was adept at putting difficult times behind her, though. "People have reasons for things. I don't believe people set out to hurt other people. Sometimes it just happens," she said matter-of-factly.

Anastasia described herself in her teen years as a "smart, but wild child" who began working summers and after school as soon as she was old enough. She and her best friend from first grade, Holly, worked together in the shoe department of the J. B. White department store where the girls shared a locker and almost everything else in life. In one of the most anguished moments in her early adulthood, Anastasia recalled her junior year of high school and the loss of her friend to suicide after Holly had been caught cheating on a test. "Getting caught meant that Holly was going to lose everything," Anastasia remembered. "And she came to me for sympathy but instead, I was so angry with her that I didn't show her the compassion I should have. She told me she loved me then she took an overdose of aspirin and died." Until the end, Anastasia readily expressed her feelings of love and appreciation to almost everyone in her life.

After graduating from high school in 1985, Anastasia attended Winthrop University "for about 20 minutes," she said, and entered into a relationship with a man that, though destined for failure, resulted in two of the best things to ever happen to her – she learned she needed coping skills and she gave birth to a beautiful red-headed baby girl, Lauren. At about the same age her mother was when she left Anastasia's father, Anastasia also left Lauren's father and began the struggle to provide for her child as a single parent herself. From operating her own typing service to doing advertising sales for a local radio station to helping a long-term boyfriend with his restaurant and real estate endeavors, Anastasia worked steadily, having little time to pursue the art that she knew was inside her.

"Anytime I could, I would go back to working with the soil," she would say, always recalling her time as a child at her grandparents' home. "It was there that I felt the connection to the earth with my hands as I dug into the top white sandy layer to reveal the dark earth below. As I dug deeper and deeper, the color of the soil would change ... I can still remember how the cool moist dirt smelled." She continued, "My Granny was passionate about her garden, and she instilled her passion in me. The older I got the more she shared with me to the point that I became obsessed with landscape design and architecture as an adult."

*

The artist's affinity for working with the soil eventually led her to start a floral business of her own specializing in unique cultivars and interesting, if not bizarre, designs. "I was 31-years-old and slowly, slowly, I finally pulled myself out of debt," she confessed. It was at her floral shop on Gervais Street that one day in the year 2000 an older gentleman walked in and ordered flowers for an ex-lady-friend. "He was more than twice my age, but he was just so adorable that I couldn't resist him. He asked me out on a date, and I said yes."

Within a year, Anastasia and Marvin Chernoff were married, but Anastasia, who suffered with a variety of respiratory infirmities, including asthma, had undergone additional pulmonary damage while working in the floral industry. She made the difficult decision to leave her floral business behind. "Also," she said, "Marvin was working part time then and we started traveling. Argentina, Uruguay twice, Chile, Italy, and eventually Africa."

It was on a trip to Botswana and South Africa, including Robben Island where past President of South Africa and Nobel laureate Nelson Mandela was imprisoned during apartheid that Chernoff first felt the inspiration to sculpt. "When I first started sculpting a world-renowned artist and very wise woman told me that she didn't start creating her greatest work until she completely abandoned her ego," Anastasia said, equating this sage advice with the lessons she learned from her visit to the places where Mandela had made such tremendous sacrifices for his cause.

"I started in concrete and moved to porcelain," Anastasia told me for my article, remembering the early days of her large format art and working with concrete, rebar, and chicken wire. She credited artist Britta Cruz and the time Cruz spent mentoring her with her move to a lighter and more malleable medium. "I am also indebted to some amazing women who encouraged me," she said, listing Lee Ann Kornegay and Heidi Darr-Hope as early inspirations.

"I'm fascinated more so by the journey of the creative process than the outcome," she said. "Once I've finished a piece, I usually have very little attachment to it and am ready to move on to another art experience. I really don't know what I'm doing and, when I first started creating, I thought that it was important that I did. After driving myself a little crazy for a while, I decided it was okay not to know. ... Inevitably, it's going to change throughout the process and, if I've already labeled it, I can be thrown off with my process which creates frustration in me."

A person with a strong appreciation for smooth round forms and a bent toward the sensual, Chernoff began sculpting torsos and female nude forms early on – some of her earliest shows focused on a number of small female derrieres in assorted shapes and colors. "The human body consistently turns up in my emotional playground, which results in much of my work being figurative. I never know what will manifest itself, which creates a surprising, sometimes humorous, and always enlightening outcome."

Anastasia's first big solo show was called *Extrusions* and was held in an upscale restaurant space on Main Street in November 2009. "I was so excited to get this show. I spent all my time getting ready for it and installing it. It was such a wonderful experience, and I was thrilled once I had it up and people began arriving to see my work," she recalled. The problem came immediately after the event when the manager of the space asked her when she would be picking up her work. "Picking up my work? I thought – I just finished installing it!" she says, remembering her shock that she was meant to take her art out of the space on the same night she moved it in.

Luckily, she had been in previous negotiations with Columbia's alt-weekly newspaper, *The Free Times,* to curate an exhibit for the upcoming Mingle and Jingle party, an art and commerce event celebrating the Christmas holidays, in the weekly newspaper's open space in the front of their building. So, she moved the *Extrusions* show to the space at *Free Times* and, at that show, she was asked to permanently take over curating the space for the monthly First Thursday art crawls on Main Street. In that, the gallery Anastasia and FRIENDS was born.

Anastasia didn't take for granted the unique opportunity she had been given. "Anastasia and FRIENDS has been a tremendous opportunity and experience for me," she said. "Showing great new artists gives me a huge charge."

Citing her early mentors as Cruz, Iona Royce Smithkin, and Steve Hewitt, the former director of City Studios on Calhoun Street, Chernoff also identified some ceramicist idols, including Sergei Isupov and Doug Jeck. "Although he isn't a ceramicist, figuratively speaking and from a realist standpoint, Ron Mueck also takes the cake." It isn't difficult to see the influence of all these artists in Chernoff's work, and her life, for that matter.

Anastasia went on to welcome dozens of both established and emerging artists into her gallery space. Rotating out artists monthly and opening their exhibitions on the first Thursday of every month, to coincide with Main Street Columbia's First Thursday arts crawl, Anastasia and FRIENDS became the starting point of the circuits we artists and arts lovers would make, mapping out a circle on Main Street that encompassed us all. There were regulars whose art showed multiple times, like Michael Krajewski, Matthew Kramer, Billy Guess, Bohumila Augustinova, and Lindsay Wiggins. Bonnie Goldberg, Alex Wilds, James Lalumondier, Toni Elkins, Paul Kaufmann, Blue Sky, Jarid Brown, Whitney Lejeune, Michael Dwyer, Kristina Stafford. The list goes on.

And there were her famous black light parties, multi-artists exhibitions, painted violins, kites, poetry readings, singer-songwriter jam sessions, and dance exhibitions and parties. Anastasia was always ready to showcase the kind of creativity you can hang on a wall or rest on a pedestal, but she was even more excited when she could use the space to midwife some innovative, paradigm-jostling way of exploring humanity. She was most in her element when her arms and doors were wide open, and she knew in her bones that something thrilling was about to go down.

*

When Anastasia was diagnosed with cancer in 2015, it was impossible for anyone to believe that she would not beat the little demon threatening her and leave its corpse on the curb with a kiss and a lesson learned. She seemed invincible. Surely her positive energy and indomitable spirit—her lust for everything life has to offer—would prevail. We all believed this for months, and she believed it, too.

On December 3, 2015, before her sixth anniversary show, Anastasia posted on social media that she was taking a break from hosting First Thursday at Anastasia and FRIENDS to focus on her health and that her dear friend Bohumila Augustinova would be stepping in to run the gallery in her absence. She wrote, "For the past six years, I've loved creating, curating, and managing the gallery at Anastasia & Friends. Our art openings are so much more than a typical opening - they are reunions, filled with old and new friends gathered to see and talk about the latest exhibition and their lives. The gallery explodes with laughter and love every First Thursday of the month as we all reconnect and share a part of ourselves with each other. It's a sacred and spiritual time for me, and to say I will miss you all greatly is an understatement. Tears are streaming down my face as I type this to you because I feel like this gallery is more than a space, it's a child we've all raised together over the last six years. ... It's been one heckuva wonderful ride, everyone. Thank you for all the incredible experiences we've shared together over the last six years. Thank you for all the love you've shown me during that journey. Regardless of what may happen to the space down the road, our energy from all the great shows and times we've shared together there will resonate forever. We're all a part of the bricks and mortar. I love you all so much - you mean the world to me!"

Anastasia fought her cancer like a fiend for another year. She remained hopeful that a clinical trial would save her and didn't give up on the possibility of something magical happening until almost the end. On a daily basis, hundreds of friends, and acquaintances whose lives she had touched sent her social media messages of love, appreciation, and encouragement. It didn't seem even fathomable that she wouldn't make it. Until she didn't.

On December 6, 2016, Anastasia Chernoff moved on to another realm and the Columbia arts community felt a punch in the gut unlike anything we had felt before or have felt sense.

Some people leave a hole in the world when they leave us and for those closest to Anastasia, those for whom she was an integral part of everyday life—Ann and Lauren, LeeAnn, Bohumila, Paul, Maria, Michael, Lindsay—there is a space where Anastasia was that will never be filled.

But for so many of us, Anastasia didn't leave us wanting. She left us with so many gifts—memories, life lessons, inspirations, new ways of seeing the world and its resources—that our baskets are full. We will never be the same not because we lost our friend, but because we had her to start with. She left her fingerprints on our spirits and our lives. She lives on as we do.

"I make art because I have chosen to live my life in the happiest place I could possibly be. Art is a huge form of exploration and enlightenment for me. I had no choice but to be an artist. I wouldn't care if I had to live off of food scraps, I wouldn't change my profession," she said in 2012. "I feel like the career choices I made leading up to becoming a full-time artist were the ones that were subconsciously chosen based on their creative components. The ability to mesh both my mind and hands gives me a sense of individuality, independence, and challenge."

My home is full of the art of Anastasia Chernoff. Female torsos, giant fortune cookies, an anthropomorphic pig face breaking out of a chicken-wire cage, long sultry disembodied fingers, and more. Like a lot of people who knew and loved her, I see Anastasia every day when I see her art. And like almost everyone else who knew her,

I see life in the way she helped me learn how to see it. Full of choices and possibilities, Full of friendships and loves that are always due a celebration. Full of art.

Thorne Compton
Remembering Thorne with Thoughts of Love and Peace

By Dale Bailes

Thorne Compton and I met at U of SC in the early sixties. We were on the Junior Varsity, of the Debate Team. We made a mutual friend of Bob Anderson and did our best to make this first black male student at USC feel welcome. That was an uphill battle in those days. I lost track of Bob after I left graduate school in 1965; Thorne kept track and even told me of being in touch with Bob's widow and child in recent years.

Thorne and I met again in the early seventies. He had done a stint in the Peace Corps with first wife Jo; I had been a hippie mail man in San Francisco, among other West Coast Adventures.

Those adventures led to my pulling together a crew of artists, Viet Nam vets, and singers and seamstresses to open the Joyful Alternative. Thorne was a regular there at our original 2009 Green Street location, stopping in for a record or a book every week, and papers. THE VILLAGE VOICE and GREAT SPECKLED BIRD, that is.

Thorne managed to function in the academic environs better than I had. He earned a doctorate and became an English professor. When I published my first book CHERRY STONES and went to work with the Arts Commission, he invited me to do poetry readings for his classes. He would go on to deanships and department chairs.

I pursued other interests—running a music hall at Folly Beach, getting an MFA in Screenwriting at USC/West. I taught in prisons and on Navy ships, and a planned two-year gig as an adjunct at Moorpark College in California ending up being twenty-five or thirty years.

At one point in the eighties, Thorne got in touch to make sure I got the scoop on Carolina's big celebration of James Dickey. He got me in, and I was privileged to see and hear such literati as Harold Bloom and John Simon hold forth.

It must have been about that time I began to make an effort to find a full-time teaching job SOMEWHERE, and I made yet another request of the most stolid academic friend I knew for a letter of recommendation.

He must have written a dozen letters, without complaint.

Until I was visiting in Columbia from California in the early nineties and ran into him at the campus bar Hunter-Gatherer. After some catch-up conversation over a beer or three, he blurted out in faux exasperation—I think—"Please don't ask me to write anymore _____ letters of recommendation!"

I didn't.

I spent a few more years adjuncting at Moorpark until I got tired of freeways and retired to live with my best friend Jo Baker at Pawleys Island. Thorne, having lost his Jo years earlier, was remarried, retired, and removed to Michigan for several years.

The odds were long that two old friends would meet again at the top of the hill where Saluda meets Heyward , but it happened. About two years ago.

I stopped at the sign and waited for a man and his dog, motioning them to go ahead.

Thorne and his dog Bo weren't taking any chances, so I rolled down the window when Thorne looked closer to check my plans. Two happy old codgers, I guess we seemed to any passersby. And although Bo tugged on the leash and whimpered about having more peemail to check, we caught up a bit. I was on my way home from my work at U of SC School of Nursing, where I occasionally was a Standardized Patient.

He didn't know the term. I explained I portrayed scenarios of different illness situations, with student nurses. The irony was thick as he managed a smile and said, "I'm the real thing." He had months, or maybe a couple of years, left.

We ended our car window conversation with a promise to get together soon for a nice bottle of red, and lots of "telling lies."

My personal lethargy, isolation at Pawleys, the pandemic…it didn't happen. Most of us have made the same mistake.

Thorne's son Chris Compton messaged me from Los Angeles that if I was going to see him again, it should be sooner rather than later. Thorne's wife Raven was kind enough to arrange a visit with him the week before Easter.

Even without a good red, we had a very good hour. We talked about Bob Anderson, the early days of Joyful, those letters of recommendation. He smiled and mentioned a memory that surprised me. "Those parties on South Walker Street. Live music and a hundred of your closest friends. Some of the best times I ever had!"

As usual, he asked what I was writing, I told him an artist named Janet Kozachek had provided two pieces of work that had inspired some ekphrastic poems. New as the term was to me, he remembered learning it a dozen years ago. I told him I would send the art and the poems.

I don't know if he was able to see the stuff before he passed. One of them, with the artwork that inspired it used with the artist's permission, is printed below. The poem, "Obeisance," has a puckish tone that I associate with Thorne Compton and is dedicated to his memory. As is the next glass of red I wrap my hand around.

OBEISANCE

The posture is apotropaic.
To appease Thanatos, back when.
And now to fend off his vengeful
Sibling, Erinyes.

It is not a conscious thing.
It is brought forth by naked fear
As pandemic stalks the land.
The gesture is archaic, bold.

Bare haunches taunt our oldest
Dread. They show contempt
For knowing time is never
Long enough, nor safety certain.

What I create may have
A longer span. A gesture, small,
To thwart some master plan.
A wrench in the machine.

So. Black-robed, grinning bearer
Of the scythe—or shrieking sister
Eris—bring forth your deadly kiss.
I here present, a target you can't miss.

Clark Ellefson
A 'ChangeBot' for the City

By Kristine Hartvigsen

Like the prominent art pieces he has created over a 40-plus-year career, Clark Ellefson is innovative, funky, minimalist, colorful, and even quirky. His brain never goes to sleep. Every line of a city building, curve of an ocean wave, texture of a birch tree, or shape of a leaf are unconsciously catalogued and stored in the vault beneath one of Ellefson's ever-present bucket hats.

One of these images might surface when he is enjoying a Rolling Rock at the Art Bar and doodling on a cocktail napkin. Or it might be retrieved as he sculpts the wooden base of one his popular lamps. Minute details may seem spontaneous at first glance, but they emerge from the catacombs of Ellefson's maze-like mind, marinated, then plucked at just the right moment from the gems tucked away in his mental vault.

A longtime Columbian, Ellefson earned a BFA (with an emphasis in sculpture, ceramics, and film) from the University of South Carolina in 1974. Early in his career, he worked for the South Carolina Arts Commission but left after an incompatible change in leadership there.

"Everything was in free fall for a while," he explains. "The agency took a different direction, and I didn't like it."

If Ellefson is anything, it is discerningly independent. He refuses to link himself with anything less than absolute quality, money be damned. He performed carpentry work to support an aspiring sculpture career. That skill set led quite naturally to designing and making furniture, a tangent that he followed with favorable results.

In the late 1970s, Ellefson formed a business partnership with the late Jim Lewis. They eventually set up shop on Lincoln Street in what then was a mostly abandoned, run-down area west of Assembly Street. It was decades before "The Vista" downtown district became the hot spot it is today.

"At that time, it was a big risk," Ellefson recalls. "We signed a five-year lease. We were both self-employed and living hand-to-mouth."

The partners – calling their business Lewis+Clark – soon forged a name for themselves creating contemporary, Memphis-inspired and avant-garde furniture. A signature Japanese kimono-shaped cabinet helped put Lewis+Clark on the map. Produced in limited number, the kimono cabinet is a collector's item now. One resides in the State Art Collection, and one sits in the office of Columbia Development Corporation Executive Director Fred Delk, a good friend of Ellefson's. The kimono cabinet briefly gained multinational repute, given a place of honor in the upscale European headquarters of a company that invited Ellefson to attend its grand opening – in Switzerland.

"I was so broke at the time," he says. "I couldn't go to the reception. That was a lost opportunity there."

Eventually, Lewis became interested in pursuing other interests on the West Coast, and Ellefson bought out his share of the company to become the sole owner of Lewis+Clark. Commissions and sales were steady for a time, and life was good. Still, Ellefson hungered for more creative challenges and found them in the unlikely visage of a tire shop on Park Street around the block from his studio. Something about it caught his eye and stirred the creative juices. So, when the Strock Tire Company closed, Ellefson and local entrepreneur Jeff Helsley joined forces to lease and convert the space into a decidedly unique, otherworldly neighborhood watering hole — the Art Bar — which opened on September 18, 1992.

"In the beginning, it wasn't just a bar to me," Ellefson says. "I saw it as a sort of laboratory" where creative minds could meet, mingle, and be cultivated.

In those early days, many people avoided the mostly dilapidated part of town, thinking it unsafe. However, as the adventurous gave it a try, word started getting out about the bar's uber-cool, dimly lit, funky interior (somewhat reminiscent of the alien bar scene in Star Wars) and the eclectic mix of punk rock, grunge, techno, rave, and alternative music wafting through its sound system.

Every design element in the Art Bar was carefully considered, with Ellefson serving as lead designer, craftsman, and art curator. Ellefson built the futuristic metal bar and harmonizing furniture himself, adding allure and mood lighting with Christmas lights, vintage lunch box lamps, and a straight-from-the-museum touch-triggered plasma globe. He adorned the walls with edgy works by local artists. There was nothing else like it.

Throughout most of the 1990s, the Art Bar quickly became the late-night destination to enjoy cocktails and blow off steam on the psychedelic fluorescent-painted, black light enhanced back dance floor. After 2000, the dance focus yielded to an emerging demand for more live music and karaoke.

At the time of this writing, Ellefson, a youthful 70, was planning updates for the popular bar. "We are renovating the bar piece by piece," he says. "We want to keep the history and feel of the bar but bring it up a notch or two here and there. ... It's been 27 years. It's time."

Lewis+Clark continued to prosper at its Lincoln Street location for nearly two decades, and Ellefson mentored up-and-coming artists, giving many of them professional exposure in his onsite gallery. He also apprenticed young artists, schooling them in the hand assembly of his increasingly popular art lamps, characterized with carved wood-and-steel bases with artisan paper shades. And it was Ellefson who organized the popular, twice annual art crawls, "Artista Vista" in the spring and "Vista Lights" in the fall, making the downtown Vista accessible to all.

With the attention came growth and prosperity in the district. Restaurants, hotels, bars, and galleries sprang up, as did the rents. In fact, by 2007, the rent on Ellefson's Lincoln Street studio more than quadrupled, forcing him out as the economic recession was taking hold.

"It was a huge tragedy for me," he says. "My landlord was a douchebag developer. … But I have always suffered the woes of leasing space and being turned out. I have always felt that if you can own your space, it is really better for your career. Artists often go into a derelict neighborhood, improve the place, create demand for it, improve property values, and then get pushed out."

A survivor, Ellefson persevered and once again established himself as an even greater success than before. Ellefson's good friend, Fred Delk, shared an opportunity he knew of. The city of Columbia had acquired a property near the Congaree River on the 1000 block of Huger Street as a possible new location for the Columbia Museum of Art. The museum had opted to relocate downtown at the corner of Main and Hampton streets, so the vacant Huger Street property was just sitting there. It had a building on it that once housed an appliance parts company. And the property was available.

Ellefson and other displaced art entrepreneurs, Mark Woodham and Tommy Lockart of One Eared Cow glass-blowing studio, formed a corporation that they named Appliance Arts Company. They purchased part of the property, and One Eared Cow moved into the existing street-front building.

"We agreed early on that they could have the front of the building because their business depends so much on retail," Ellefson explains. "Most of my sales are out of state."

Ellefson built onto the original building, adding 6,000 square feet of workspace and meeting space to receive visitors. The structure sits behind One Eared Cow and is accessible by the parking lot off Huger.

Taking the live/work concept to heart, Ellefson designed and began building an outwardly minimalist, standalone structure housing a one-bedroom loft home just across the parking lot entrance to his new studio. By the time he finished the building and moved in, it had been transformed into a showplace of sexy postmodern craftsmanship, from its hand-hewn kitchen cabinets to its inlaid wood floors stained in multiple contrasting colors and the staircase with hand-cut decorative accents.

During the time he was laboring on his studio and new home, Ellefson often glanced wistfully at the barren lot to the west, adjacent to his studio and backing up to the Congaree River. Where others saw weeds and arid soil, Ellefson saw potential for a professional artists' colony on the site.

In the summer of 2007, Ellefson convened folks from the Columbia Development Corporation (CDC), the Columbia Design League, the SC Arts Commission and the City of Columbia for a two-day meeting to gather input from members of the local arts community on the potential planning, design, and ownership structure of art studios and live/work units being proposed for the 1.5-acre plot. The dialogue begun that summer originally was known as the Columbia Art Studio Project, or CASP. Later it became popular to refer to the project as "Stormwater Studios." In the end, which was the name that stuck.

"The focus at first was on a pure studio building split into bays where artists could purchase a space," Ellefson recalls. "Each bay would be 600 to 800 square feet. For a lot of people, which is plenty of space. And there would be covenants in place to ensure that the space was always used as an art space."

Those ambitious talks begun in earnest unfortunately stalled the following year. Stormwater Studios seemed to be going nowhere. The land, still owned by the CDC since 1984, remained undeveloped for about a dozen years. Then it was announced that Vista Studios and Gallery 80808, a magnet for the Vista since opening in 1990, would be closing. The signs had been there. Artist studio rents went up. Available gallery space shrunk to make way for expanding neighbors. Lease agreements became increasingly tenuous.

"Stormwater Studios got in the quicksand with the recession," Ellefson says. "What got it out was the Vista Studios being threatened. It was going to go away. The landlords decided they wanted to do something different with the space. That was the stimulus to reignite the Stormwater Studios project."

Stormwater Studios opened in the spring of 2018 and has proven to be a destination in the Vista for art lovers, particularly during Third Thursdays, the district's monthly evening gallery crawl. The gallery at Stormwater has had a successful series of events and shows since it opened. Ellefson noted that fundraising was underway for Phase II of the development, a structure capable of accommodating industrial sized fabrication projects for welders and sculptors.

The now-historic COVID-19 global pandemic, social distancing, and related closures that began for the United States in the spring of 2020 slowed progress on Phase II but plans at the time included the possible relocation of the 701 Center for Contemporary Art from Whaley Street to the Stormwater Studios site in Phase II. Ellefson said the pace of that project ultimately would depend on fundraising and how the post-pandemic economy recovered.

If financed, a third phase may house loft-style living spaces, interactive outdoor areas for the public and a short walking trail.

Pandemic living did not hamper Ellefson's work on multiple projects. The uber-contemporary, modular home he designed and built directly faces his professional studio off Huger Street. It was not an issue to simply walk the few steps over to his studio and work in complete isolation.

"I was able to work non-stop. There were no distractions," he says. "I did miss my recreation time at the Art Bar and going out to eat and things like that, but I always have plenty of work here."

One thing is clear. Gentrification will not compromise his live/workspace or Stormwater Studios. Ellefson and Delk saw to that.

"We wanted to create a permanent space for artists," Ellefson says. "The artists rent from the CDC, which is dedicated to keeping the property a community art resource. That is what makes it work."

While working to get Stormwater off the ground, Ellefson continued running Lewis+Clark full-time AND working on something new ⊠ public art installations. The first, called "The Gong," was dedicated in 2015. The sculpture commands attention from under a canopy at Lincoln and Senate streets near the Columbia Metropolitan Convention Center. It is a tribute to the beloved late advertising guru Marvin Chernoff.

He went on in 2018 to complete a special commission for Studio 2LR, an architecture and design firm in downtown Columbia. There were both functional and aesthetic reasons for the assignment. The firm's new office tended to flood during heavy rains, and they figured cisterns could be a solution. But why not make those cisterns art as well. Two birds. One stone.

Studio 2LR then approached Ellefson with the idea of making their double cisterns a unique installation of public art. Ellefson had long installed a series of mood robots throughout the Art Bar and was beginning to craft smaller, desktop-sized versions as "ChargeBots" that doubled as charging stations for household devices. They had been selling well, and after some discussion, the firm's leaders decided they wanted Ellefson to tap into his robot muse and make the Studio 2LR cisterns into a giant GirlBot and GuyBot standing sentinel outside the building to gradually funnel away excess rainwater.

Incidentally, the ChargeBots were literally stealing the show for Lewis+Clark in 2018. "They are more popular right now than the lamps, and they've gotten national interest," Ellefson says. "When I was at a design show in Santa Monica, the *LA Times* put the ChargeBots in an article citing the best designs in the show."

In 2019, Ellefson completed construction of a new reception desk at the Columbia Museum of Art. He is enjoyed the artistic alliances that came with that project.

"It's fun for me and interesting. It's a different dynamic to partner with other people," he says. "I have been collaborating with others on several projects. The museum job, which was an interesting project."

In early 2020, Ellefson completed his latest public art sculpture, "Green Eyes," a continuation of the "robot" series that helped transform the Studio 2LR site. The artwork is a cock-headed robot face emerging from the ground with, you guessed it, glowing green eyes. "This sculpture narrates a long-ago fantasy of when robots walked the earth and serves as a cornerstone to the Vista's River Studio Arts District," Ellefson said in a Vista Guild article announcing the unveiling. Green Eyes, therefore, represents a long-buried member of the robot family who has emerged from the ground to be discovered.

In four-decades-long career, Ellefson has never participated in an art opening quite like that of Green Eyes. The unveiling on April 17, 2020, was — by pandemic necessity — a "drive-by" event, with viewers cruising by and honking their horns in approval.

"I stood out there waving at cars. Some people stopped and came over to look at it more closely, but they kept their social distance," Ellefson recalls. "It was fun."

In contemplating the future, Ellefson is realistic. "I have gotten a little older," he notes. "I'm 70 now. Do I really want to run around the country doing craft shows? It's a lot of work."

What about retirement? "My 'retirement' has meant slowing down to 40 hours a week," he quips. "I am still trying to do that."

The shift in focus to sculpture and public art suits Ellefson, whom countless city officials have called a pioneer for awakening positive development and growing the arts in the area.

It is true. Ellefson is a visionary — the visionary who dreamed up the Congaree Vista arts district at a time when it was decidedly not chic. Now his vision has come full circle and is beginning even to lap itself with new creative sparks that continue to emanate across the city.

WILLIAM PRICE FOX
SOUTHERN VOICE, NEW YORK SPIRIT

By David Axe

William Price Fox was a famous novelist and humorist and part of the literary clique that got *The Village Voice* really up and running back in the 1960s. But I knew him as a mentor and friend much later in his life, when he was in his 70s.

I was a writing student in the graduate English program at the University of South Carolina in Columbia when I first met Bill in late 2000. He took a liking to a short story I wrote. As I sat there in his cluttered office with him, he called Dan Cook -- then the editor of Columbia's *Free Times* newspaper -- and told Dan he should assign me some articles.

Dan graciously agreed. That was the start of my professional writing career, which has taken me all over the world for *Free Times* and many other publications. I even got to write for the *Voice* for a while before that storied newspaper shut down in 2018.

Bill was a Columbia native, but he talked a lot about the *Voice* and his years in New York City. How he and his friends would go to Windows on the World, the restaurant on top of the World Trade Center, for a beer and a corned-beef sandwich.

"At night from the booths on the north side we could see the moving necklace of lights on the Eastside Parkway, the Westside Parkway, the George Washington Bridge and the Bronx Whitestone Bridge," Bill wrote. "During the day we could see the Peregrine Falcons that had first found a home in the cliffs of Rockefeller Center but had discovered the Twin Towers and had decided to stay."

"It was a glorious sight and if you were a poet, you became more poetic. If in love, more in love. And if you were in trouble, you probably stayed that way but now you were much more aware of it.

Prose like that made Bill a great teacher. He wasn't much of a lecturer, but he didn't need to be. He could just read his old stories, novels and screenplays and you'd learn by osmosis.

Bill wasn't just a great mentor. He was a great man. Deeply humane, powerfully honest, and empathic to a rare degree. On the morning of Sept. 11, 2001, he trudged into class, said, "Well, this is awful," and, with sorrow in every line in his face, told us to get the Hell out, go home and watch the news.

Looking back on that morning, I deeply appreciate that Bill didn't try to be a "leader" or an "example" as our towers fell, and the world ended. He acted how he felt. And how he felt was sad and confused. He gave us permission to feel the same way. He trusted us with our emotions.

Bill later wrote about that day in his sporadic column for *Free Times*. "On Sept. 11, when the cameras were showing us the disaster, I couldn't help watching Greenwich Village in the bottom of the frame for things I never dreamed had meant so much to me," he wrote.

"I kept watching for places I'd lived: Perry Street and Bleecker Street and Charles and West Fourth and Hicks Street in Brooklyn Heights. I kept watching for The White Horse, The San Remo, The Lion's Head, the little park on 12th and the newsstand at the Christopher Street subway stop across from the United Cigar Store."

"And then I knew why I was watching. I was watching to see if I could see myself. But I also was watching and wondering how I would feel if I were at the newsstand at that moment, looking south on Seventh Avenue and facing the unalterable fact that the Twin

Towers of the World Trade Center are not only gone forever but are also the funeral pyre for thousands of New Yorkers."

I could contrast Bill's example that that of another writing teacher I was studying under at the same time. An award-winning Australian novelist, this teacher – unlike Bill – didn't trust us to feel.

In the days following the terror attacks, she tried to manage our emotions. Control them. She went around the room asking each of us what we were feeling, then passed summary judgment based on our responses. "That's right." "No, you're wrong."

You can imagine who was a greater comfort in those red days.

On Bill's passing in 2015, his son Collin wrote a lovely essay exploring his father's deep humanity. It came in part from the pain of losing his four-year-old son Wyatt to cancer in 1973, Collin explained.

"He kept that perspective hidden far from sight," Collin wrote. "The only time he let it slip came in a farewell letter to an Iowa newspaper."

In that letter, Bill described a day shortly before his little boy died. He recalled the hot air balloons that were "floating in across town just above the big oaks and the elms."

"A rainbow-colored beauty came sliding in towards our house and I decided that if Wyatt and I followed it he would get well again. I picked him up and strapped him in and with the top down we headed out directly underneath."

"Most of the time he could look up at the roaring colors above and he was, for the first time in a long time, and probably for the last time, really laughing."

"And then the balloon started drifting south. And as it did, suddenly a south road appeared that I could follow. The balloon drifted south for a while and then east for a while and each time it shifted, the roads kept shifting with it. It happened over and over again and as it did, I really believed that everything -- the balloon and the roads and the sun and Wyatt could and would hold on forever."

They didn't. Nothing does. Bill understood that. It seasoned every word he said. Every story he wrote. Every relationship he had with a struggling young writer.

A few years later, a refreshingly optimistic Bill wrote passionately about a young politician he was convinced would become America's first black president, and a transformational force for America. He was right. He was almost always right.

When, in 2000, Columbia residents battled state politicians over the racist Confederate flag flying over the statehouse on Gervais Street, famous historian Shelby Foote, a white Mississippian, unwisely chose to weigh in. "I treasure Confederate heritage greatly," wrote Foote, who at the time was 84 years old.

Foote's comment perhaps betrayed the biases of the community he grew up in. At least that's what Foote's defenders said. But Bill, just 10 years Foote's junior, wasn't having any of it. He declared Foote "a second-rate novelist and third-rate historian."

Never say Bill was afraid to speak truth to power.

Thank you, Bill, for your wisdom and generosity. Your wife wrote that you passed away surrounded by your cats. I'm glad for that. After all, I've got a bunch of cats, too. They're a writer's best friends. You didn't teach me that, so I had to learn it on my own.

Phillip Gardner
My Favorite Story

By Jon Tuttle

For more information about Phil Gardner, please visit his website.

The first thing you'll learn is that he'd rather not have a website. "I feel a little uneasy about all this," he says on his homepage, posing casually beneath a menu featuring his biography, books, and music. I suspect his wife Tressa put him up to it. She's his number one fan and kind of his business manager and helps him reconcile the practical need for exposure to his personal "desire to be invisible." "I was born in the previous century," he says, making it sound like the 19th. "I know things are different now."

She'd really like you to know about him. He's happy if you don't.

Of course, if you live around Florence, you can't help but notice him: he looks exactly like nobody else. Meet him for a drink on the porch at Apple Annie's Pub, and you'll see what I mean. When he steps out of his silver Miata and comes striding toward you, everyone will look because, damn, who the hell is *that*? He's got, for one thing, a shock of white hair he's had since his twenties and still keeps long because who the hell wouldn't? He's got, for another, an inimitable sense of style. Whereas most people put on clothes, Phil gets *dressed*. Today it's a gauzy white Otavalo mountain shirt, black jeans, and black boots, because, as Tressa says, "he's really one of the only people who can get away with it."

And boom: that's when you'll recognize him. He's *that* guy—the front man for Felonious Funk, a Florence-based horn-powered dance and party band covering a wide range of soul, R&B and classic rock artists like Stevie Wonder, Steely Dan, Little Feat and The Eagles. For twenty years before that, he sang lead for the Woodys, the Pee Dee's house band, a regular attraction at bars, festivals, benefits, and really great wedding receptions.

Here's my favorite Phil Gardner story: I walk into Southern Hops, a Florence brewpub, while the Woodys are on stage. There's Phil out front, givin' it away, belting out maybe "Saturday in The Park" or "Domino," and as I pass through the crowd, he points at me and follows me with his finger, thereby making me for six breathless seconds the second coolest guy in the joint.

So okay: here he comes, across the porch to our table. People stop him to say hello because, hey, I know you! You're that guy! He'll make his way over, his eyes smiling, always smiling, but before he sits, he'll extend his hand palm up, always palm up, and as you take it, you'll feel like the second coolest guy in the joint. He'll order a bourbon on the rocks and another round of whatever you're having, and so will begin the best conversation you've had in months, because as you speak, he'll look directly at you, always directly at you, because there's nobody more interesting over your shoulder or across the room. And at the end, if you're not paying attention, he'll pay the whole tab.

Here's my favorite Phil Gardner story: this is back when we were both between wives and would head straight from work to this very pub. This one particular afternoon a woman I know comes over and joins us. Before she knows it, she's having the best conversation she'd had in months, and by the time he's paid the whole tab, she's obviously smitten. So smitten, it turns out, that she goes home, tracks down his phone number and calls him, just to chat, from her bathtub. Again: she calls him, that very same night, *naked*, from her *bathtub*. I'm pretty sure she thought he was Mick Jagger. Everyone thinks he's Mick Jagger.

But Phil doesn't want to be Mick Jagger. He was not born to sing lead, nor did he aspire to it. It was just gradually thrust upon him. "I gotta tell you," he says of the person he becomes on stage, "I don't know who that guy up there is, really. I can tell you that it's totally expressive, that it's a response to being surrounded by music. When he opens his mouth, he's never sure what's gonna come out. It's about joyfulness."

Phil's actually more like Charlie Watts: happy to sit in the back and carry the beat. His start in music came in fact as a drummer with an R&B/beach band when he was fifteen. "In my heart of hearts," he says, "I've always been a drummer. Think about it: its physicality, its centrality to the band—it's protection from the world. The drummer is at the center of it all, but he's not in the spotlight."

Before going off to college—this was in the 60's— his brother Michael taught him to play guitar, but "at the time, I didn't care about being a performer. I wanted to be a songwriter." He earned a bachelor's and master's at UNC-Charlotte, then found his brother again. "It was songwriting that brought Michael and me together in his Raleigh studio in the early 90's, and because he wanted to record the songs I'd written, I was expected to sing them. Because I was not an accomplished player, I became the lead singer. I was forty years old."

With Michael and some friends, he formed The Gardners of Soule, a band specializing in their own songs, and toured clubs in North Carolina. They cut CD's, about fifty songs on four disks, sixteen of which received Honorable Mention in *Billboard's* Annual Song Contest. Those disks are still available and remain close to his heart because the nights spent in the studio "were, for me, magic. And never before or since have I enjoyed the generosity and kindness from other artists that I experienced with those four guys."

Phil got his start in music growing up just outside Goldsboro, the grandson of Depression-era tenant farmers. "And they all could sing," he says. "It was gospel in my mother's family and mostly country and western in my dad's. My dad's brothers were guitar players. And both families were great storytellers too." The cross-pollination of music with storytelling has informed his sensibilities as a writer, which have placed him, if you believe Ron Rash, "in the first tier of the South's finest short story writers," and which have won him the South Carolina Academy of Authors' Fellowship in Fiction, the Piccolo Spoleto Open, and (three times) the South Carolina Fiction Project. One story has been adapted to film, another nominated for a Pushcart Prize. He's also written five screenplays, because sometimes his ideas "express themselves as movies in my head, and I truly love the experience of writing scripts."

Last year saw the publication of his fifth collection, *Where They Come From, Where They Hide*. Like many of his stories, these are populated by denizens of a thinly-disguised Darlington County who wander through the Paradise Lounge--the black hole at the center of his fictional universe—when they're not chasing each other down Highway 52 or running at night through a swamp full of cottonmouths.

Here are my favorite Phil Gardner stories: "Neighborhood Watch," from *Somebody Wants Somebody Dead* (2012), in which good people for good reasons drop a pillowcase full of kittens into Black Creek. Or "Things That Smell Like Food," from *Available Light* (2013), in which our protagonist stands handcuffed watching his Subaru Brat full of rabbits get towed away, while at home his wife anxiously ovulates. Or "It's Usually This Dark By Now," from *The Future Never Lasts* (2015), in which our narrator gets talked into committing murder by an angel with scars where once were wings.

Or "Vibes," from his first book, *Someone to Crawl Back To* (2001), which begins with a woman buying a vibrator at a garage sale (yes), then shooing her husband off to play golf. Later, he's in the attic, going through all the detritus of their life and having his suspicions. At the end, the story finds in a perfectly brewed cup of coffee with just the right amount of sugar an apt metaphor for a happy marriage.

Vibes are, for Phil, what make a good story; whatever they are—a current, an aura—they're what beguiles a reader to keep reading. A vibe is a "hard thing to describe" he says, "but you know if it is or isn't there. It's the atmosphere that surrounds every aspect of the story. It's what moves us. I don't know that I can separate vibe from setting. The Darlington stories are essentially about an imagined setting, but that place is inseparable from its tragi-comic vibe."

Sometimes plot, the selective stacking of incidents, can beget vibe, as happens in my favorite Phil Gardner story, "Murmurs." It was based on an article he read in *Newsweek* about a guy whose new artificial heart valve made dinging noises when he got excited. In Phil's story, the valve becomes a rhythm section when the narrator—a lonely guy, with scars--holds a microphone to his chest during a karaoke contest and thereby slays the room. He ends up in bed with a girl who, because she is deaf, didn't get the joke, but who lays with her head on his chest, murmuring, "I can feel it. I can feel it."

In such stories, Phil's characters frequently achieve a sublimity they cannot name or even apprehend. But they can feel it. They cannot appreciate how particular incidents have shaped the tragicomic arc of their lives. But they can feel it. And so can the reader, and that, says Phil, is how art works. "A song is only half a song until it is heard." Writers need "an audience to complete what they've created by participating in that creation; strangers who willingly open an unfamiliar door and walk inside." Both forms, he adds, are "primal. They take us places unreachable by any other means. They champion feeling over reason."

Phil's consciousness of his craft is the rather astonishing product of his childhood. He grew up in a family that told stories but did not write them; he remembers that notion as "impermissible." But he recalls his grade school spelling tests as opportunities to "use words to organize sentences that told a story." His aesthetic began to from when he was fifteen and would lie on the floor, one speaker on either side of his head, listening to the Beatles' *Sgt. Pepper's Lonely Hearts Club Band*. "I listened to that album two or three times a day," he says, "and when new instruments were introduced, I'd shine a light on each. I studied three things: Selection, Arrangement and Emphasis. Aristotle had other, better words for these concepts, but as a way of organizing choices—what to put in, what to leave out—they cover a lot of ground, whether you're making a story or a song. Or a life."

I told you this would be a great conversation.

So, look now that he's gone to pay the tab, I'll tell you my favorite Phil Gardner story: the one where he proposes to Tressa. For two years, they had looked at one another across various dining rooms and dancefloors and thought: damn, who the hell is *that*? At each encounter, the exchanged the same pleasantries, except with deepening subtext. Finally, they met for a date right here at Apple Annie's, where the conversation was so good, they decided it might be pleasant to continue it someplace else, so they followed each other someplace else. Along the way, at a busy intersection, she stopped at a red light and looked at him in her rearview. He looked back. And she looked back. And he looked back.

It was a long light.

And then, at the same moment, and you cannot make this stuff up, they both got out of their cars, rushed quickly toward one another, and that's not actually how he proposed. How he proposed was: one afternoon about five years later, she was driving down Highway 52 toward Darlington, with him following in his car, and she looked up and spotted a billboard. It had a diamond ring on it and read, "Tressa, will you marry me? Phillip."

It took about a half-mile for that to register. Then she pulled over, and they both got out of their cars again.

They were married in 2001 at the president's mansion on the campus of Francis Marion University where, until his retirement in 2016, Phil was Mick Jagger. He was the founding director of FMU's Writing Center and a popular but exacting professor of English. He received the university's award for Distinguished Research and Scholarship and has been a regular speaker at high schools, universities, writers' series, or retreats. He's also won a raft of awards you can read about on his website.

These days, Phil and Tressa divide their time between their homes in Darlington and North Myrtle Beach. As opportunities allow, they visit his son Hunter, a Clemson graduate now living in Brooklyn, and daughter Maegan, a UNC alum now in Winston-Salem. He continues to perform with Felonious Funk, and she works at Florence/Darlington Technical College as Associate Vice President of the Southeastern Institute of Manufacturing and Technology. They grow their own vegetables in the back yard and are happy to give you some but would rather have you over for a cookout with some great music. You won't need to bring anything. They've got everything.

Most days, now that he's retired, Phil arises early, brews a perfect cup of coffee with just the right amount of sugar, and pours them both a cup. He'll see Tressa off to work, then go upstairs to write. Sometimes, instead of working on a story, "I'll write letters to my three granddaughters. I can't tell you how satisfying that is." Later in the morning he'll go for a walk, then have lunch and do some reading, maybe play guitar, or take a nap. In the evenings, when Tressa's returned, they'll make dinner together.

"Tell me," he says, his eyes smiling, "that's not the greatest life in America."

And that's my favorite Phil Gardner story.

Tyrone Geter
Enduring Spirit

By Claudia Smith Brinson

Tyrone Geter makes people weep. Sometimes they stand before a monumental drawing of his, overwhelmed by the feeling that they know this person, not in an ordinary sense but a heart sense. Sometimes they stop almost unwillingly, startled into acknowledging that someone is gazing back with familiar eyes, is just like them. Sometimes they pause -- and cry at the ways of the world and the ways not quite of this world, at the offering bowl at the feet of a homeless man, at the blood vessel-leaf vein-tree root-beehive hair of a contemplative teen.

Geter does this with line and charcoal and chalk and erasers, the skin, hair, and clothing in infinite variations of black, white, and gray. He does this by intensifying the human gaze, directed straight at you, not exactly confrontational but unavoidable even when the eyes are somewhat hidden. He does this by working larger than life, a head-to-thigh portrait five feet tall, a full portrait eight feet tall.

Maybe he does this as a mystic, able to produce ley lines on paper. Certainly, he does this as a master draftsman skilled enough to trust even his first mark.

Fellow artists speak in superlatives. "On the street we would say he has a 'monster talent,'" said painter, lithographer, and University of Georgia professor Joseph Norman, comparing Geter's draftsmanship to Leonardo da Vinci's. "Tyrone is one of the greatest living draftsmen." Painter and sculptor George Danhires, a former Ohio University classmate, agrees. "He is a great draftsman; no one in the country can hold a candle to him." As does Boston painter Paul Goodnight. "I think Tyrone will probably be legendary."

Geter, 75, was born in Anniston, Alabama, then a town of 30,000 with steel mills and foundries, an Army fort and depot. In 1961, a white mob in Anniston firebombed a Greyhound bus carrying Freedom Riders, clubbing the civil rights activists as they escaped the fumes and fire. But by then, Geter and a sister had joined their mother in Ohio.

During Geter's early years, grandfather Augustus Phillips worked as a barber and in a steel mill; Grandmother Lizzie Phillips cared for their twelve living children. "We lived in a house where nobody went hungry, but nobody had money," said Geter. On their way to and from school, the youngest children ran and fought their way through a white neighborhood, besieged by attacks on their three-mile journey. The older boys worked as golf caddies on a nearby segregated golf course. The older girls and women cleaned and cooked for white families, crossing the course to reach their employers. But an uncle who served in the Navy returned home to insist, "Someone has to go to college."

Geter's grandmother agreed, and the family met, pooled their funds, and sent his Aunt Doris to Miles College, a historically black school in Fairfield, Alabama. Geter's mother, Gussie Mae, named after her father, also hoped for a better life. She headed North.

"My mother, she was never scared," said Geter. "Also, too, that Underground Railroad that she hopped on, she could do it because we had cousins who left the South for Ohio. She had a base." Her education had ended in the third grade, and, in Dayton, Ohio, she was again a domestic worker, but her son attended college. He enrolled through his mother's canny bargaining. She told a white employer that she wanted the funds for her son's first year. She met objections by pointing out that no taxes or Social Security had ever been paid for her work. She was owed.

"Her position was her kids were going to move past her," said Geter.

Geter's environment had told him that art was something on the side. He had been intrigued by sister Liz sketching cartoons, guided by "Draw Me" ads on the backs of comic books. And at Rochester High School in Dayton, his art teacher wrangled him back into class when he considered taking driver's training instead. He was named, at graduation, the "most outstanding artist of the year." But no one he knew made a living as an artist. "Back in those days, I was lucky to do it. Nobody thought about art as a career at all." Expecting to be a teacher, he chose art education as his major, until a class assignment to design costumes and reenact Humpty Dumpty propelled him to studio art.

In and out of college in the 1960s, needing work for funds to return, Geter was drafted and served in the U.S. Army in Gunzburg, Germany. Afterward a more serious student, he earned his Bachelor of Arts and, by 1976, a Master of Fine Arts from Ohio University in Athens. On the Athens campus, black students confronted white students who attacked them; successfully – and peacefully, with announcements at classroom doors – arranged a memorial service for Rev. Dr. Martin Luther King Jr.; almost won a battle for a campus workers' union; campaigned for and obtained a well-funded black studies program; and initiated an African relief movement.

While the poverty and racism of Alabama in the 1940s and '50s constrained Geter's early years, his college years introduced him to the theories and actions of empowerment: to King's "unarmed truth and unconditional love," the Black Panther Party's "all power to the people," and the African National Congress's "non-racialism." For Geter, "College allowed me to become a little more educated." On the other hand, "I think all my training came from all the people surrounding us."

He had landed at "one hell of a progressive school." South Africa had banned the African National Congress (ANC) in 1960 and imprisoned leader Nelson Mandela in 1962. South African

Lindiwe Mabuza -- a poet, anti-apartheid activist, and later a diplomat -- taught history and literature at OU from 1969 until 1977, when she went to Zambia as a journalist for the ANC's Radio Freedom. South African Cosmo Pieterse -- a poet, playwright, and critic exiled in 1965 -- taught at OU from 1970 until 1981, when he was refused re-entry into the United States after a visit to London. Geter also absorbed the lessons of scholar Rod Bush, who argued that the black worker stood in the "centrality of the struggle" against capitalism and white supremacy.

Mabuza held dinners at her home for the African and the African American students and the celebrities passing through. On a visit, Geter's life took another turn, a romantic one. Hauwa Tini Adamu passed him on the stairs. "She was going up the stairs, and I was going down. If I had been five seconds earlier or later, I would have missed her. That's how fate works." She was there to help her sister, a graduate student expecting a baby. Mabuza arranged a chaperoned first date, and the next day Adamu left for Nigeria. She returned six months later. "I had thought it out; my life would be really, really bad without her," said Geter. At 26, he married.

Geter worked for a minority cultural center serving black and Hispanic residents in Lynn, Massachusetts. "We had a rally there for this black youth; he was really beaten badly. Nothing happened. We took to the streets. We had this huge rally. Then I wrote an article, too, about the failure of politicians to do what they were supposed to do in this case. I said we should let them feel the 'hot wind of change.'"

For Black History Month, he was organizing again, bringing in as speakers Margaret Burnham, a civil rights attorney and the first black woman appointed to Boston's city court; Fleeta Drumgo, one of three Soledad Brothers, black inmates charged and acquitted in a Soledad Prison murder; and Angela Davis, a Marxist feminist professor charged, jailed, but acquitted in connection to an armed courtroom takeover aimed at freeing the Soledad Brothers. Within a few days Geter was fired for his organizing. He tried working at a food stamps office, where he quickly earned promotion from technician to supervisor but quit within months. "I couldn't do art. That job ripped me apart inside, seeing people suffer all the time."

Next, he taught art part-time at Framingham State College, in Framingham, Massachusetts. In 1979, with the assistance of a humanities grant, Geter accompanied his wife to her home in Zaria, northern Nigeria. They stayed for seven years. Geter taught art at Ahmadu Bello University. He immersed himself in the culture of the Fulani, a nomadic and Muslim ethnic group, and his wife's people.

He drew -- 100 drawings in his first year -- and he painted – vivid village scenes of cooking, washing, play, and celebration. Sketching the baobab tree obsessed him. A strange and magical "upside down tree," baobabs store thousands of gallons of water in enormous trunks while witchy bare branches resembling roots reach skyward.

In West Africa Geter met the American jazz musician and composer Yusef Lateef, who asked Geter how he created. The ensuing conversation led Geter to decide his ability-- going straight to the paper or canvas, no preliminary sketches, and making a mark -- came as a gift from his subconscious. An idea arrives; Geter listens. "It comes from inside of me; there's very rarely any preconceived notion," he said. If an idea does not capture him, he awaits its return, changed and with resonance. "It's an emotional thought, and I can't do it until I run across the center of the thought, and when I see it, I know it. And then I build everything around that.

Before leaving for Africa, Geter had begun drawing very large, mostly solitary figures stretching past life-size to monumental. He admired Francisco Goya, whose 18th-19th century drawings, paintings, and engravings portrayed rulers and their wars and exposed corruption and violence; John Singer Sargent, likely the most celebrated and prolific portrait painter of the 19th-20th centuries; and

Charles White, a 20th century painter, printmaker, and civil rights activist who depicted African American life. But "I never studied anyone to be like them," said Geter. "My entire life I wanted to see if I could be who I was. I've always been willing to struggle to learn something."

Even so, he was intrigued by their ability to transcend portraiture and make emotional and political statements. "We both want to ask questions," said Charleston artist Colin Quashie, who uses paint, collage, and installations to comment on race. "It is our job as artists to ask the question, to put the mark in a certain way. And then you take yourself out of the equation and leave a point of view." Norman calls Geter both a poet and a samurai in that regard, diagnosing and evoking the beauty and despair of human existence with such perfect ability and control that each stroke does what it should.

In 1987, during Nigeria's economic collapse, the family – two daughters richer – returned to Ohio. Geter taught at the University of Akron and began illustrating children's books, including "Irene and the Big, Fine Nickel" by Irene Smalls and "White Socks Only" by Evelyn Coleman. At ten books he paused, feeling he was asked to draw the same little black girl over and over. Few American artists are full-time artists; fewer still make a living wage. Almost half seek multiple sources of income, reporting less than 10 percent comes from art sales, according to a 2018 survey. Three-quarters make less than $10,000 a year from their art, according to a 2017 survey. Geter kept teaching, coming in 1999 to Benedict College in Columbia, South Carolina.

In 2003, Tini Geter died instantly of a stroke; a few months later Geter underwent triple-bypass heart surgery. He stopped making art, bitter from loss, but forced himself to recover when he saw that he could destroy the rest of his family. "I had to get up," he said.

Throughout these years, Geter's interest in and expertise with line grew. He still painted but charcoal had become his signature. He left on paper lines he had abandoned; he tore lines through torsos. At some point, he ripped his paper, unhappy with a mark, then returned the paper, adding layers in collage, creating depth, and challenging the art's edge. That extra dimension expanded again. In front of artwork, he placed items – a tricycle, an offering bowl, paper doll chains, a shopping cart. "In a series called 'The Art of the Misdirect,' Geter challenged the race politics of the hoodie with torn paper embracing young men's heads and upper torsos to become feathers, headdresses, and cloaks. The Columbia Museum of Art (CMA) acquired "I Don' Old, I Don' Tire, But I Ain't No Ways Don,'" in which layers of a magical tree and bird emanate from the head of a hard-worked woman.

Tall, bearded, soft-eyed, with a habit of putting a hand to his heart while speaking, Geter has never painted a police beating or a lynching. But he has always been political. "I learned early making political statements is one thing, but how you make them is another. I learned not to beat people across the head with it. Most of my life I've been searching for a way to make a statement but allow people to enter the statement and move in their own direction."

He believes, "What I have to do is make people feel. What this society does that we live in, it breaks that down, that sense of oneness with the human race. I want anybody walking past my work – you have to feel, you have to feel you couldn't just walk past."

His titles announce such intentions: "Bull's Eye" and "Calling Me a Bitch Won't Make You a Man" in the series "Ain't I a Woman," "Mother Nature's Last In-House Domestic Servant" in the series "Black!" "My Beauty Is Not My Beast" and "What's a Mother to Do, #1 and #2" in the show "Enduring Spirit" at the CMA. He credits his own mother with this aspect of his work. "I feel a responsibility for everybody. My mother raised me that way, that I was responsible for every person that walked on Earth. You couldn't walk past something and not see it. If you saw it, you had to try to do something about it. That's how she raised us."

Other cultural institutions exhibiting his work include the Florence County Museum in Florence, South Carolina; Hampton University Museum, in Hampton, Virginia; the Museum of Fine Arts and the National Center of Afro-American Artists, both in Boston; and the Butler Institute of American Art in Youngstown, Ohio. He won the 2016 award of merit at the competitive ArtFields in Lake City, South Carolina; a 2019 Elizabeth O'Neill Verner Governor's Award for the Arts from the South Carolina Arts Commission; and a 2019 residency at the famed Yaddo artists' community.

In May 2020, Geter has pinned three incomplete drawings to a wall of his upstairs studio in Elgin, South Carolina. Retired from Benedict, he has more time for art. In one drawing, a terrible and beautiful storming sky consumes the paper. In another, a tornado heads toward a child who addresses us, the people who have made this likely. A wrecked tricycle sits before us on the floor, a harbinger of children's future as an endangered species, the tentative series title. "He'll have a loose idea and start something, and it will evolve and takes you along on a journey," said Danhires. "Like da Vinci, he tells a great story," said Norman.

Terrance Henderson
Friend and Hero

by Jason Stokes

Henry Longfellow is credited with saying *"We judge ourselves by what we feel capable of doing while others judge us by what we have already done."* This encapsulates the subject of this article because others look at him with awe and wonder at all that he has accomplished, while I know he always feels capable of doing/creating/expanding his immense talent and his library of work constantly. His talent and his creativity are only matched by his loyalty and friendship, of which I get the honor and privilege of receiving and accepting. Allow me to introduce you to one of my best friends and creative heroes, Terrance Henderson, aka T.O.

Our paths first crossed around 2000 (hard to believe that is more than twenty years ago) as we were both helping to judge/score middle schoolers who were auditioning for the drama program at the high school level. Through trivial conversation in between auditionees, I came to realize that we were both the same age yet somehow to me he seemed more seasoned, more accomplished at his chosen crafts than I. When he told me of his love for the show *Dreamgirls*, I was smacked in the face with where I had seen him on stage, as he had recently closed at Workshop Theatre. While the exact nature of our conversation is fuzzy (after all it has been twenty years), I recall telling him just how engaged I was in his portrayal of Curtis, the smarmy producer who pushes Effie to the background while making personal and professional moves on her sister Deana, because I rarely leave a production having any real visceral reaction to a character. However, after seeing T.O.'s performance, I had true disdain for him... not just the character, him. This has always stuck with me even all these years later because now that he is my brother and one of my closest friends, I know how truly immersed he was in the role of Curtis, a trait he brings to all his work.

Our paths continued to cross sporadically over the next few years, but our lives changed in the summer of 2006 when we were both cast in the Workshop Theatre production of *The Full Monty*. I had seen T.O. serve as both a choreographer and director on another project but I had never worked in a show with him, never played opposite him and I now had a front row seat to this artists craft. Based on the 1997 movie of the same name, T.O. played Horse, an elderly man who loves to dance, is out of work, perhaps in need of an attitude adjustment, who joins a ragtag band of other unemployed men who are going to perform a striptease to make some quick money. Watching him transform night after night into a 60-year-old dancing man was the stuff of inspiration. His mastery and creativity were present from the beginning, snatching any and every tiny nuance he could to put on his character and, if it didn't work it was gone just as quickly. One particular moment that always stands out regarding his attention to the smallest of details; in the musical number *Michael Jordan's Ball* all the Monty Men are "playing" basketball. In a shoot around of sorts Horse goes up for a rebound and lands slightly off kilter causing his knee to buckle slightly, an issue I'm sure anyone over 40 can associate with. It was a tiny nod of realism that probably washed over the audience, but I got to see this reaction night after night, always at the same time in the song, always with same implied reaction from Horse… "Damn it! My knee again." He added a companion reaction later in the number as there is a fast break for a quick score and, as Horse was no longer that spry, he simply allowed the others to flow past him as he gave a simple forget-about-it wave to the passing crowd. I learned from these moments that no detail in live theatre is too small to be overlooked or under supported.

It was this same year that we began a collaboration not only in my film work, but in his dance company as well. At the time he was Artistic Director/Choreographer for Vibrations Dance Co. I would tape his performances (*Sista Girl and the Soldier, Echoes & Images, Ninacity, Experience in Rhythm*) not only for him to review but also to give him a high-quality video catalogue of his work. Over the last fourteen years we have morphed into a collaborative unit that combines the live theatricality of dance performance with multi-image/video/film elements, culminating with his 2014 original work *The Blackman...Complex*. This work was not simply a live performance with background imagery, it was a truly personal work that combined singing, dancing, poetry, history, racism and above all the human condition.

T.O. had a concept in mind for the film/video elements and how they would interact with his live performers, but he was unsure how to make it happen...which is where I was lucky enough to enter the equation. He would write or block a specific scene the way he saw it in his mind, we would talk about the logistics and potential problems, then we would go out and shoot. At every turn as I edited the vignettes, he would watch the cut, ask questions, and actually listen to my answers. Sometimes when an artist creates a new work and then allows someone to collaborate... there is no real collaboration as the originator never truly wants to share control or ideas. It can degrade into a tent-pole situation where each camp sets up apart from one another and never budges or listens to what the other camp might have to offer/critique. Perhaps that's what makes us such a good creative team. At no time did I ever want to overstep my boundary with a piece of work so personal to my friend and, at the same time, he wanted to use my knowledge and expertise to make his vision, his dream better. In the end, though still and always his creation, there was so much "us" in the finished product that I still get goosebumps reminiscing about it. I got to help create a piece of art that was not mine, from a place I could never know on my own, and work with someone brilliant enough to know when to ask for an opinion.

Rarely does an actor get the opportunity to work with their close friends on a show that is life changing, rarer still is to do it twice.

But it happened for us in 2009-2010 when we were both cast in the Trustus production of *Rent*. Because of the successful December/January run in 2009-10, the theatre brought us back to open the 2010 season as well. In our city it is a rare privilege to actually improve on a classic show by taking what you and your castmates have done and build on your own creation instead of building off the Broadway versions of characters. We had the opportunity to add to our own character arcs and backstory to create an even more original take on this classic piece. It was during this production that T.O.'s strength was ever so prevalent. You see, his father had passed away that summer just before we were to begin rehearsals. He never missed a beat, and he never missed a rehearsal. Theatre is home and art his therapy. As he was playing Collins, there was one line he had to sing towards the end of the show "I can't believe he's gone." We were a few weeks from opening and as he came to this moment all of the family that happened to be onstage realized that this line had taken the breath out of our friend. We gathered around him like the entire cast at the series finale of *Mary Tyler Moore*. Our arms all around him. He did not shrug the gesture away, he did not ask for a minute, he did not apologize for his grief. He simply let us all be one, united in pain to help share the load. Sometimes the strongest need to be lifted so they can be reminded they are not alone.

I was accepted into the 2015 Second Act Film Festival and, as I was going to be shooting my film as well as directing, I knew that I needed an extra set of eyes to assist me. I asked T.O. if he'd be willing and without hesitation he agreed. The cast was small and there was only one location, I was trying to keep things simple. However, on the day of the shoot, I was swallowed up by the technical aspects of making the film and, as such, lost sight of my story's dramatics and characters. All I was concerned with was did my camera move work, was it in focus, was the balance right in the frame. Smartly I called to my assistant director T.O. how a certain take was. He came down from video village and pointed out that my actress, who was playing a mute, had made a gesture with her hands over her heart, signifying the importance of her point. I got up and, with T.O.'s help, adjusted the movement in the scene to match what she was "saying" with just simple gestures. Without him and his eye for that small detail the moment would have been less impactful. Artist reciprocation at its finest.

In 2016 I was offered the chance to direct a show at Trustus Theatre, *Tail! Spin!*. As I had never directed a stage play before, I was unsure of what would be asked of me and if I could even do it. After talking with my wife, I called T.O., and I asked him one simple question: Can I do it? I barely finished the sentence before he said "Yes." Then he followed his statement up with the important question: Do you want to direct it? From that statement forward I read the script as a story that I wanted to tell not simply be a part of by acting in it. Reading a script with a director's eye is very different than reading with an actor's eye. T.O. and I have a very similar trait when we are working on a stage show in that we rarely write anything down. We keep what we are working on inside us, so it remains a part of us during and through the creative process. It was T.O. in fact who stated "...if I write it down it's kinda like it's no longer a part of me." Well in directing this show I HAD to write everything down because I was thinking for the entire cast by putting my ideas, my vision into their minds so they could graft themselves into their characters and in the end, all create the same universe to play in.

Once the show was mostly blocked, I asked T.O. to come and watch our first stumble through. Having been on both sides of the stage I didn't have to tell him what we didn't have or what will be coming (I confess I broke that rule as well by prepping him before the run started). All I wanted from him was his honest opinion about the story I was telling and if any of it felt out of place or misguided. Once the run was finished, we retired into the rehearsal space at Trustus to chat about the show and he, being one of my best friends, had a largely positive response to the work. But he also had several small things that he mentioned, those little minute details that needed to be added or cleaned up, just as he'd done with his Horse character a few years earlier, to make my universe and the universe my actors were creating more alive, more real. I do not remember the specifics of his notes, but I do remember when I told his notes to the cast it was received and incorporated into their world.

To date, my friend Terrance Henderson is still working on his craft. Still creating new stories to tell and new avenues to tell them. He has been working/singing with his group Indigo Soul on a new show aimed at young adults about the importance of realizing they matter, that they have a history to share and a path to blaze, *Shine,* he also performs regularly with The Columbia Rat Pack with Kevin Bush, Jonathan Jackson, and me (important note: we don't impersonate the original Pack. We just continue their philosophy of life, which is to sing a little, drink a little, and have a whole lot of fun). We have been performing as The Pack for almost fifteen years and, each time we get together it's like picking up a favorite book from where you left off and the rollercoaster ride continues without missing a beat. Words cannot express how much I enjoy singing, kidding, roasting and cutting up with my guys…and how much we enjoy taking the audience on the ride with us.

In the simplest of terms of my friend I shall only say this; my life as an artist and as a human being is more complete because of the artist known as Terrance O. Henderson. This city and state benefits greatly simply by having a creative spirit like his in its midst. It is true that a work of art is subjective but in my humble estimation, there is no question that T.O. Henderson is a work of art that should be treasured by all. It has and shall continue to be an honor and privilege for me to work with a true artist and one of my best friends.

Robert Burke Kennedy
Tornado Maker

By Ed Madden

> "Life imitates art far more than art imitates life. This results not merely from life's imitative instinct, but from the fact that the self-conscious aim of life is to find expression, and that art offers it certain beautiful forms through which it may realize that energy."
>
> –Oscar Wilde, *The Decay of Lying*

Every party had a theme.

There was the Easter party where everyone had to wear a hat or bonnet, and we played croquet in the cemetery next door. There was the superhero party where Wonder Woman told everyone to watch out for her invisible plane parked on the front lawn. There was the oxymoron party and the "come as your own motif" party—no one knew what to do with that one. At the "come as a cliché" party, a woman wore a plastic horse dangling between her legs and the man with an ice tray affixed to his shoulder won for lamest costume. Yes, of course, there was a costume contest. Bert and I won the faculty division. We took a friend who was visiting from Austin and the three of us handed out pink dollar bills with a portrait of Eleanor Roosevelt where George Washington should be and a numeral three where there should have been a one. Robert Burke Kennedy—Rob—the host of these events, swirled through the house in a bright orange shirt and shiny red pants, affixed over his crotch a small basket onto which he had glued 15 or 20 tiny doll hands. He was, he laughed, *going to hell in a handbasket*.

When I met Rob, he was a graduate student in the English Department at the University of South Carolina, where I was a recently hired faculty member, just out of graduate school myself. The house in the Cottontown neighborhood of Columbia was a large rambling wreck of shag carpet and bad smells and a rotating roster of graduate student roommates. There was a long hallway across the back of the house, bedroom doors opening off the hall like a dorm or a boarding house. At the front door there was a massive and once grand set of stairs leading to the second floor, but there was a sheet hung over the stairs—the landlord forbade anyone from going up there, for safety reasons I think—so Rob and his roommates used the stairs for storage, boxes stacked in the ascending darkness behind the curtain. There were rumors of bats.

Some of the parties had signature cocktails, each with a name. I remember the Aqua Villa at one summer party, vanilla vodka blended with frozen watermelon, seeds removed. It was sweet and slushy and pink and easy to have too many. Later, when Rob had started catering, there would be some insanely beautiful or delicious or rare thing to eat, something he was trying out before offering at an event—a chocolate cake covered in sugared violets, or *the best pimento cheese ever*.

When I think of Rob, I think of those parties. I think of the swirl of people and drink and laughter and costumes, and I remember Rob, the whirling dervish of creative energy at the heart of it all.

Rob was an artist—that's the reason I wanted to write about him for this collection—a fiction writer and a ceramicist. He studied creative writing at USC with now deceased Southern humorist Bill Fox and ceramics with Virginia Scotchie, as well as working on staff at the McKissick Museum and running a small side career as a caterer. After he left Columbia for Atlanta, he worked in a series of high-end art and vintage furniture galleries and started his own small company of bespoke lamp design—tongue-in-cheekily dubbed The Coalition Society—which offered one-of-a-kind lamps made of slabs of Lucite, massive limbs of driftwood, a leather bustier, a lazy looping ribbon of hand-worked wrought iron.

Virginia Scotchie calls Rob "a maker." I tell her about the parties, she tells me about the energy he brought to the ceramics studio. "Everybody else," she says, "had to live up to his creativity." She describes Rob as one of those people "who made any event magical and unexpected." His creativity extended to everything he did. Those parties suggested the creative community that orbited around Rob, the community he created, and the way that life itself was for him an art, a performance with a constantly improvised script. He made art, loved art, collected art, connected artists to one another. When he announced a party, everyone had to live up to his creativity. He taught us that anything can be made better with a garnish, an accessory, a drink, a flower, a suffix, a name. A party was always more interesting with a theme.

My husband Bert and I have a small collection of Rob's pottery. Impressed on the bottom of each piece is a tiny stamp of a pear, Rob's mark. We bought three Saki cups at a student art sale, perfectly thrown white porcelain with a thick and glossy black glaze. There's also a pale blue lidded jar—more decanter than jar, my husband says—with a separate matching cup. The jar lid, which fits flat inside the lip, has a fake spout for a handle that also serves as built-in shot glass. It is like nothing you've ever seen, and the craftsmanship is flawless. Our favorite piece is a piece he gave us, a gift, a small dark silvery-gray vase shaped like a tornado. These became his signature pieces, tornado vases he called them, a form he explored through a series of organically sculpted swirls of clay thrown on a wheel. These vases swirl out and up from small bases, his fingers shaping whorled and irregular walls, the rims uneven—despite this they are steady, balanced, will hold a fistful of flowers. Ours is a small one, about four inches tall.

In the right light, the outside glistens silver; the inside is dark, the eye of a storm.

*

Rob asked me to serve on his thesis committee. I had heard his work at the irregular readings the MFA program hosted. His stories were mostly written in a deadpan voice that was clearly his own. He was a master of dialogue, of exterior expressions that revealed darker interiors, his stories often revealing things *only* through dialogue. He experimented with form, sometimes made-up words. At the cliché party, there were three or four women in hideous pastel bridesmaid dresses (always a bridesmaid, never a bride)—*hidulene,* Rob called them, one of the words he would occasionally coin by adding an *-ene* suffix—hidulene, ridiculene, fabulene. It was as if that was those were their ugly stepsister names, Ridiculene, Hidulene. Years later, my husband and I would find ourselves laughing, referring to some *Design Star* or *Project Runway* creation as *hidulene.*

Rob was a storyteller, and he was wicked funny. He told stories in such a way that they seemed to be absolutely true and also absolutely appalling, though when you recalled them later in the car on the way home, you wondered. He also had this way of hunching his shoulders and pulling his hand up as if to hide his grin, so that whatever he had just said, however innocent or banal, felt suddenly scandalous, and you were special, you were in on the joke. His eyes lit up, his eyebrows lifted, he smirked like a devil in some old Victorian cartoon. Often, the story really was scandalous. Or it provoked you, poked fun at some established idea or famous person. He loved to tell about meeting Elton John in a gallery, that when he shook his hand it was greasy with lotion. Rob would shake out his hand as he finished the story, as if slinging off the slime of it.

I remember brunch one Sunday at the Gourmet Shop, one of his whirlwind visits back to Columbia. He told us matter-of-factly that he had been raped. We were shocked. He said he had hooked up with a hot guy the night before, but that when they got to his place, he basically held him down and raped him. It hurt. We asked what he did, did he call the police? He said no, he had just emptied the guy's wallet on his way out as he left quietly that morning. The rapist was paying for breakfast he said. We didn't know what to say.

His thesis—I can't remember the title—was a *bildungsroman*, the story of a boy growing up in Michigan, slowly realizing he has psychokinetic powers and then slowly losing them as he goes through puberty. His powers dissipate as he realizes another kind of difference, that he is gay, the magical difference of childhood becoming the more difficult difference of high school and college, and the novel moves from a kind of sweet magical realism to a realistic story about a group of friends growing apart. It was as if, as a child, he could emotionally control the world somehow, he was connected to it, but as he grew up, he lost control, lost connection, and slowly began to grow away his friends. As a kid with psychic powers, the boy never does anything violent or mean. In a fit of rage, he stacks the books in everyone's lockers, so that when they open at the bell the hallways are filled with scattered books and personal things, the private contents of their lockers spilled into public. The boy only realizes after it happens that he made it happen. It's like Stephen King's *Carrie* if Carrie were sweet. And funny. And gay.

Though Rob published some short fiction, he never published the novel. I tried to publish an excerpt in an anthology on masculinity, but my co-editors refused. It was a short passage set in a house shared by six friends just before graduation weekend. They are an odd but seemingly tightknit group. They are in some way types—the smart one, the popular one, the gay one—but Rob renders them as rich characters. "Two of us were Jewish," he writes, "three Catholic. Denny and I were Irish. Half of us were rich. Half of us weren't. We lived together in a big house on Michigan. We'd all been friends since freshman year of high school, some of us all our lives."

In the excerpt, the main character, clearly a version of Rob himself, is waiting outside the bathroom. "The door was shut. I was about to knock when I heard voices inside." He says he was going to just go back to bed "when the content of the conversation forced me to stay and linger outside the bathroom door where on the other side two of my best friends chatted, one naked in the shower, the other half naked at the sink with steam filling the air and the sound of water falling and the scent of soap and shaving cream." He clearly longs for the kind of intimacy and freedom he senses between them, two men comfortable with their nakedness and their conversation. "It was just a normal occurrence," Rob writes, "no more strange than any other." One man describes ejaculating on his girlfriend's stomach, then licking it up and kissing her.

In a rare moment of interiority, Rob concludes the scene:

> I went back to my room and wondered why no one ever talked to me like that. It was such a familiar banter and nothing in Mark's voice indicated that he was revealing something sacred or sharing something secret. Nothing in Eric's seemed surprised, and nothing about it was strained. They were just talking as friends and there was nothing unusual about the conversation, except to me, its nature. I realized that even that, for them, was nothing out of the ordinary. But it was a conversation I would never have. It seemed not to be intimate, but there was an intimacy between Mark and Eric that I would never have with them. I decided that if I'd allowed myself, there would be many, many more, far too many, situations like that. I put it out of my thoughts."

The scene is heartbreaking. In a book about masculinity and male experience, I had hoped this story would raise questions about the possibilities and impossibilities of intimacies among men, but my co-editors were disturbed by the explicitness of the young men's conversation. I loved the title Rob gave the piece, "Lingering, Outside." *Outside*, wanting to be inside, wanting this ease and openness and familiarity with another. The scene establishes a desire for intimacy and a resignation that some forms of intimacy may never be possible. *It was a conversation I would never have.*

Ironically, Rob got people to confess things. Rob did this to people, told stories until they found themselves telling their own. It was a performance but not a one-man show. He created communities of intimacy and startling honesty among his friends. Everyone was expected to play a role in his unseen and improvised script. You were never embarrassed. The spotlight moved around the room, briefly on you. Once, he was housesitting for another professor and hosted a small poolside party. There were drinks and stories spun out and laughter and suddenly we all learned that the very quiet, very handsome, very straight law student swimming with Rob in the pool—they were the only ones in the water—liked to have his girlfriend insert her finger in his rectum when they had sex. He grinned, holding himself steady in the deep end of the pool, his wet black hair pushed back, his eyes dark. Rob backpaddled to the shallow end.

*

Rob was incredibly funny. I asked my friend Ray McManus, who was in the MFA program about the same time, what he remembered of Rob. "All I remember about Rob," he texted, "was that he always cracked me the fuck up. Didn't matter what was being discussed, he just had something snarky and outrageous to say about it." Ray adds that Rob was one of the first people he met in graduate school, "and I've always been thankful for that." Rob included you, he charmed you. For a man who wrote so movingly about being excluded, he had a talent for making you feel part of his circle.

One of his longtime friends, Zinnia Willits, says that whenever you were with Rob, you were laughing. Back then Zinnia Weise, a graduate student in the Public History program at USC, Zinnia was one of the longest of Rob's roommates in that rambling party house. They stayed in touch as he went to Atlanta, and she got married and went to Charleston to work at the Gibbes Museum of Art. She says he was "one of those friends who just pick up the phone and start talking, no matter how much time has passed." When she would go to Atlanta for museum work, she knew that she would go out with Rob, and she knew that "whatever we were going to do, I was going to have fun. I was going to laugh."

Rob was energy, he was full on. "Rob always did things full steam ahead," Virginia says. "*Everything* was interesting to him," Zinnia says. She tells me about a Halloween party they went to as 1920s flappers. He went to a traditional African American hairdresser in Columbia to get oiled finger waves in his hair. "He wanted to go all the way," she says. Bert remembers Rob's quest for the perfect pimento cheese recipe. He tried every restaurant in town. *Every single one.* He needed to sample every possibility before he could perfect his own version. "He would go to TK Maxx," Zinnia laughs, "and he wouldn't buy just one sweater, he'd buy 15." She says she would push back sometimes at moments like this—he needed friends like that, someone to keep him in line—and he would snap, "Don't talk to me like that."

Zinnia reminds me that Rob's room in the house was a mess, a disaster, clothes thrown everywhere, towels on the floor. When we visited him in Atlanta, he never let us see his apartment, saying it was a mess, he couldn't let us see it. But, as Zinnia says, "he would always come out looking fabulous." There was public Rob, party Rob, put-together Rob, the Rob that presented to the world, but there was also private Rob, messy Rob. I mostly remember public Rob, I remember how excited he was to be included in one of the photo spreads of the Atlanta social scene in *Jezebel*, a glossy lifestyle magazine. But Zinnia reminds me that sometimes he would stay in his room for days. The roommates would just tell each other, "Oh, Rob's not engaging with anybody right now."

"Everybody expects the fun from you," she says, "but there was a darker side always right under the surface." Behind the shiny surface there was darkness, a quietness. "As much as there was fun and lightness" to him, she says, "there was always something heavy in the background."

Zinnia describes quiet drinks on the porch at the old house with Rob, just them. "It was times like that that I loved him the most," she says. "He wasn't performing for other people." I loved that Rob, too. I remember a quiet Sunday brunch in Atlanta at his latest discovery, a barbecue place. We were in town for a conference. This was our chance to see him, just before we left town to drive back to Columbia. We had drinks—something with mescal, I think. We sat in a booth, he leaned into our conversation, making us laugh. He was subdued, but still charming. Rob walked us to our car, and we hugged, hard. It was the last time we saw him.

*

Only a month or so before he died, Rob returned to Columbia as a visiting artist in Virginia Scotchie's BFA and graduate ceramics workshops. A couple of Virginia's students had met Rob when they accompanied her to a gallery show she was part of in Atlanta, a show Rob helped organize at the Marsha Wood Gallery, one of the last places he worked. She says the students fell in love with Rob, as one does. Zinnia says he was starting to make a name for himself as a designer. His bespoke lamp workshop in a friend's pool house was turning into a design career. The students begged Virginia to bring him back to USC; they wanted to hear about his life.

Virginia says she asked Rob to present his own work—the ceramics, the lamps—but also to talk more broadly about art and life, about making a living as an artist. Rob offered generous critiques of student work. He talked with her students about his life, she says, "his artistic ways of being a person and loving art and caring about the people that make it."

Later that fall, Rob's friends and family put together an endowed scholarship fund in his memory for an outstanding USC undergraduate student in ceramics. The gift agreement calls Rob a natural ceramicist, whose work combined technical proficiency "with a flair for the dramatic and whimsical." I think of that jar lid that looks like a decanter spout but serves as a shot glass. The agreement says that one of his greatest joys was to be asked back to USC as a visiting artist by his beloved ceramics professor, Virginia Scotchie. The agreement states, "The Rob Kennedy Scholarship will be in perpetuity at the University, so young ceramic students will always know who this fabulous and fashionable free-spirit was who lived his life in the never-ending pursuit of inventing and producing 'uber-elegant and glamorous' design."

Before he left, Rob bought one of Virginia's student pieces: a foot being pushed into a shoe that was too small, a shoe it would never fit.

*

Rob is the only person I've ever known who seemed like a character from Oscar Wilde—his sense of mischief, his creativity, his incessant and biting wit, his pronouncements. He was given to making pronouncements. He told Zinnia, not long after he met her: "Zinnia, you can't drink pink wine." He would look at her before they left the house, declare with a shudder, "*What* are you wearing?" "I was like a project of his," she says. He took her to Metropolis, the gay dance club in Columbia. "He would just throw me into situations," she says, "and see how I would react."

I remember one evening Rob wanted to teach me about cocktails. I grew up fundamentalist, never drank anything with alcohol until I tried beer in graduate school. I knew nothing. He decided I should sample things on the menu by their names, sample drinks by their color. Names of things mattered. We tried greens. We tried something that tasted like a liquid Jolly Rancher candy, too sweet. Rob made something up that the bartender was happy to mix for us. don't remember what it was, just that it was strangely green and delicious.

Rob was the usher for our wedding, when we decided to marry in 2005, ten years after we'd begun dating and ten years before it would be legal in South Carolina. Rob showed up too late to usher in anyone but Bert's sister. They walked down the aisle, the two of them smiling and waving like celebrities. All eyes were on him, he was wearing something stunning. He changed outfits for the reception. Bert reminds me that there were, in fact, three costume changes, another outfit for dinner. Debra laughs when she remembers him walking her down the aisle. "He was so fun."

As a wedding present, Rob gave us a wall pocket made of blue and purple blown glass. We love early twentieth-century pottery, and I've always loved ceramic wall pockets, vases you could hang on the wall. Rob convinced the artisans at One-Eared Cow glassworks to make one for him, for us. It is a beautiful thing. To our knowledge, it was the first and maybe only one they ever made.

Zinnia says at her wedding he turned his jacket inside out during the reception, because the lining was beautiful, and "he wanted everyone to see it." She said he was the talk of the reception. When he died, friends and family who didn't know him called her; they all remembered him from the wedding.

There was a portrait of Rob in the back hall of that Cottontown house, a painting that was unfinished. I don't remember the story about the artist who painted it, someone from back in Michigan, I think, an artist from his college years. He later damaged it in a move and tried to repair it. They had it on an easel at his memorial. It seemed more beautiful because it was unfinished. It seemed more beautiful because it was damaged.

I always thought of Rob as incredibly resilient.

He was artist, wit, compère, host extraordinaire.

I always felt lucky, special, that I was the only faculty member invited to most of his parties.

When Rob came back to Columbia, he never gave us notice, at best an email or phone call the night before. We would have brunch somewhere and he would tell us outrageous stories. You knew if you were with Rob, you would be laughing. You might be drunk; you might be with people you'd never otherwise meet. (How did he know the gay porn star?) You might hear stories you weren't sure were true. (When did he work as a model?) You might be at some amazing restaurant. and you would certainly realize at the end that you were paying. You might find yourself walking out of some Atlanta club after dancing all night, the morning sun just coming up as you head back to his apartment. I was trying to remember if that was New Year's Eve or after Atlanta Pride. No, Bert reminds me, that was just an ordinary weekend with Rob.

Rob died in his apartment on June 19, 2016, at the age of 45. Friends knew something was wrong when he didn't show up for a gallery opening, he had helped to organize.

At the memorial service there were tons of flowers, including a large set of red lips made of roses, a tribute from his plastic surgeon.

At another memorial later that fall, held at Mary's, one of his favorite cocktail bars in Atlanta, people played voicemail messages they had saved. "People saved his voicemails," Zinnia says, "because they were so funny."

I want to start this essay all over again: whenever you were with Rob, you were laughing.

At that long ago Easter party, Rob wore a blousy white shirt and rather than a hat a small crown of flowers, like a Greek god in Edwardian garb, like someone totally out of place, An anachronism. The reason we were all there.

"The final revelation," writes Oscar Wilde, "is that lying, the telling of beautiful untrue things, is the proper aim of art."

The three black Saki cups were made for a couple and a visiting friend. We have never used them.

I am grateful to Zinnia Willits and Virginia Scotchie for sharing their memories of Rob with me.

Jillian Owens
The ReFashionista

By Cindi Boiter

On October 11th, 2021, Columbia lost one of our shining lights—a light not just in our city, but on our city—when Jillian Owens, 39, died after a year-long battle with ovarian cancer.

Jillian was a gifted and prolific writer who, as a teenager, moved from Russell, KY to South Carolina where she graduated from the UofSC with a BA in Theatre and English.

If you didn't already know Jillian for her whimsical personality, fashion sense, and sense of humor, you heard of her, for sure, when she turned her passion for thrifting and fashion into a world-wide phenomenon via her wildly popular blog, The ReFashionista. Jillian would scour thrift stores for cast-offs, often challenging herself to choose the least loveable pieces she could find—'80s power blouses, "old lady" housedresses (Jillian "felt funny" about this term but couldn't land on a better description—we all knew exactly what she was talking about), ugly sweaters, even her own unused wedding dress—and use her special magic to transform one woman's trash into her own treasure. She carefully detailed her work in words and photos and published each project on her blog complete with before and after photos, usually using herself as the model.

The artist gained international attention when, in 2012, she took on the self-assigned challenge of upcycling a unique thrift store fashion-find every day for a year. Actually, she rounded up the days in her year to 366 and she gave away every new fashion she created saying, "I don't form emotional attachments with clothing. Clothes are fun, but ultimately, they're merely things. Objects have never held much value for me. I usually tend to value experiences instead."

A virtuoso at the art of making the most drab and useless items, whether fashion for the home or body, into something both beautiful and valuable, Jillian began her ReFashionista blog in 2010. By 2020, she had acquired more than 22,000 followers from all over the world including Australia, Japan, France, the Czech Republic, and more. Many of her followers thought of Jillian as so much more than a cyber personality, confessing their secrets, dreams, and insecurities to her always open heart and ears.

"You are the best," one follower wrote. "Thank you for sharing because you are definitely helping others and are inspiring all of us."

When, in January 2020, Jillian wrote about repurposing an old Free Times newspaper box into what she called a Little Free Library for her neighborhood she was inundated with comments, suggestions, and thanks. "I smiled all through this post," one follower wrote. "And I find I am delighted every time I see an email for a new blog post from you. The little libraries are a terrific idea and a nice addition to any neighbourhood, I am sure. Good for you for being involved with your neighbours!!"

Another shared, "Once again, you have turned something hideous into something absolutely adorable (let alone useful and fun). You are one of a kind. If you had your own TV channel, I would watch you all day long."

In fact, Jillian did spend some time on television. Her status as a refashioning icon earned her appearances on *ABC News, Good Morning America, The Rachel Ray Show,* as well as features in *Buzzfeed, Bored Panda, the Associated Press,* both French *Cosmopolitan* and French *Elle,* and a dozen more cultural outlets.

On August 1, 2020, she shared the news with her followers, many of whom, despite the distance, considered her a personal friend, that in addition to demonstrating how to turn a shapeless floral dress into a mod top with a scalloped hem that day, she would also be writing about a "tumor named Clyde" that had been detected in her abdomen.

Within weeks, Jillian was diagnosed with Stage III Ovarian Cancer. Loyal to her followers though, she continued her refashioning projects, intermixing blog posts about her creative transformations with posts about life on chemotherapy.

On August 25, 2020, after the removal of a tumor the size of a small watermelon, the Refashionista wrote, "The thought of not surviving this and leaving everyone and everything I love behind so soon guts me way more than an eight [inch] incision on my abdomen did…. I'm trying to be brave, but I'm just **so. freaking. sad.**"

She completed her chemotherapy later that year only to discover the cancer had returned in July 2021.

In 2019, Jillian had married Brian Morris, having won a free wedding from the UofSC College of Hospitality, Retail, and Sports Management. Even after more than four years together, like most of her family of friends, Morris struggles with pinpointing the source of his late-wife's inimitable uniqueness, though he tries.

"I want everyone to know that it isn't just hyperbole when I say that she truly loved the people she kept close to her. This woman would do anything for anyone to make sure that they were happy and felt loved," Morris says.

Karen Stewart points to Jillian's creativity as the source of her individuality, saying, "anyone could learn how to sew, but her ability to look at an article of clothing that most people would deem as trash and see a vision of something beautiful was an incredible talent. She did that with people, too. She could look at any person and see beyond the outside and find the thing that makes them interesting. She acknowledged everyone's worth."

Phillip Higgins, who met Jillian 13 years before her death when she was singing karaoke at Vista Lights with a group of children gathered around her, says, "She was that friend we all need. The one who is always up for anything, whose humor and care-free approach to life serves both as inspiration to those around her and as a safety net, always there waiting to catch us when we fall or need encouragement without judgement."

As much as anything, Jillian was a diplomat for the city of Columbia, Erin Tyler says. "She loved how Columbia has grown for the better over the last 15 years and she always made sure to do her part to make it a better place to live."

Dan Adams agrees, "Jillian loved Columbia and it loved her. She took castoff and old things and improved them and gave them new life. She was a positive creative force, a great friend, and a wonderful human. She will be dearly missed."

(A version of this essay appeared in the author's Further Consideration column in the Post and Courier Columbia, November 17, 2021.)

LESLIE PIERCE
COMMUNITY MAKER

By Ed Madden

What I remember most about Leslie Pierce was that lovely smile, her easy laugh, a chuckle like a clear ripple in the air. (Can't you hear her?) Or the way she so easily pulled you into conversation in the lobby of the Columbia Museum of Art, or that moment she pulled out her notebook at Drip, ready to talk about her latest idea for getting people together. *Community* and *collaboration*, words that get tossed about in the arts community, but ideas Leslie Pierce believed in, lived, made happen.

Ray McManus and I were talking about Leslie, and we agreed that we were and are deeply grateful for all of the ways she made the CMA a place for writers, like that long ago Frisson series she worked on with Charlene Spearen, inviting writers to respond to work in the galleries. We're both back in the CMA next week with 40 or so middle school writers. Leslie made that possible.

She got people into the museum, she got people talking about art, but I also think she had a pointed sense of humor — as when she asked me a few months ago to give a gallery talk on Norman Rockwell, knowing full well it wouldn't be sentimental homage. She liked getting folks to see things differently — most recently through those Unique Perspectives programs, with all sorts of artists leading their own idiosyncratic tours of the galleries. She asked me to do a queer tour of the permanent collection last fall during one particularly rowdy Arts & Draughts — not only a delight, but also, I think, indicative of how she wanted the museum to be a welcoming place for *everyone*, queer folks included. She scheduled films for gay pride week (and asked me to give a lecture on the history of fag hags). This was everyone's museum.

In my office, I have two pieces she made for a show we did together with Alejandro García-Lemos, a collaboration around the iconography of Saint Sebastian. Both are collages, one a traditional image of the saint stuck in the middle of an old French ad for cameras. *Ne perdez pas votre temps!* Don't waste your time. The other a beefcake model posed before a stained-glass window, a quite physical saint. Both are so indicative of her quirky sense of humor, her expansive aesthetic, of the ways that she could pull quite disparate things — and quite different people — together.

Leslie was sweet and generous and inquisitive. She made me feel good about my work. In my email box, one of the last emails I got from her: "Will you be around this summer? Want to work with me on some programming?"

I do, Leslie, I do.

Kathleen Robbins
Glory Through Her Lens

By Tim Conroy

> "Great Art is an instant arrested in eternity."
> –James Huneker

I cannot write about Kathleen Robbins without making it personal, without including a part of my story. One of her gifts is what she brings out in others.

In her role as professor of art, coordinator of the photography program at the University of South Carolina, affiliate faculty of the Institute for Southern Studies in the school of Visual Arts and Design, and in all levels of studio art photography, Kathleen promotes the work of her students. She encourages her students to use an unhurried and reflective approach. She teaches students to question their work while giving them the space and time to develop their own voice.

Kathleen is a renowned photographer whose work integrates lyrical documentary photography with technical expertise. While attending Millsaps College in Jackson, Mississippi, and after the usual undergraduate trial and error, she discovered what she was meant to do—then worked and studied to perfect it. After college, she received her MFA from the University of New Mexico.

Kathleen has exhibited her photographs in numerous galleries and museums, including the Halsey Museum of Contemporary Art, the New Orleans Photo Alliance, the Light Factory Museum of Contemporary Photography & Film, the Weatherspoon Museum, the John Michael Kohler Art Center, the Ogden Museum of Southern Art, the Addison Gallery of American Art, the Southeast Museum of Photography, the University Museum at Ole Miss, the Columbia Museum of Art, and the Baum Gallery of Art at the University of Central Arkansas. Her work has also been featured in print magazines, electronic journals, and other forums such as *The New York Times*, *Oxford American*, *Garden & Gun*, CNN, NPR, *Flak Photo*, and *Fraction*.

Kathleen's distinctive gaze (where she aims her camera) comes partly from the long-sighted and enduring women of the Mississippi Delta, a landscape that has witnessed daily beauty and survived flood and drought, economic boom and bust, births and great loss. Her visions and textured perspectives are seen through the eyes of a diarist, personal and autobiographical.

*

In 2014, my wife Terrye and I moved into a 1928 brick in the Hollywood Rosehill neighborhood near the University of South Carolina campus. We sold the duplex we shared with Terrye's sister Deborah after she lost her eight-year battle with melanoma. We crossed over the Congaree River as the sun descended on our caregiver efforts, bringing memories and ashes with us.

Crepe Myrtles line the border on the east and west sides of our small front yard. Our screen porch faces south where in the distance we can trace the outline of the Congaree River bluffs; a view that gives depth to our perspective. A hybrid tea rose bush recently planted in memory of Terrye's mom is heavy with pink blooms. For us, the past has never been disconnected from soil or horizon, from milkweed or monarch. I believe it is this shared connection to memory, to family, to place and ground, that attracted me to Kathleen's photographs. Her images resonate like kitchen table conversations about unpaid bills, the preacher's hair, or needed shoes.

Shortly after moving onto our new street with its quirky mix of students and faculty, professionals, and retirees, we met Kathleen, her kind husband Ben Madden, and their effervescent young son,

Asher. We did not know it yet, but we would fall in love with them and our other cherished Pinewood friends.

Then in June of 2015, my neighbors Chuck Lesser and Angela Materer invited me to a presentation Kathleen was giving at the State Library as part of the South Carolina Center for the Book series. Her lecture was on her book of photography, *Into the Flatland*, which explores her familial ground, memories of kinswomen, and generational plantings of time that both connect and conflict her with a past of promise and heartbreak.

Kathleen's grandmother, Jessye, had been a filmmaker, a painter, a photographer, a keen recorder, and in spirit and size, part Kathleen. In the preface of her monograph, *Into the Flatland,* Kathleen wrote of a book that once belonged to Jessye: "*One Thousand Beautiful Things* is a collection of poems and essays, and, on an index card in the front cover, my grandmother personalized the book with a note to me explaining that this was among her favorite possessions." Jessye also wrote, "Please love it as I have and keep it always." Her grandmother had suffered great loss and this book somehow had helped her. After Kathleen finished graduate school, this note was partly what compelled her back to the Delta.

Kathleen's natural presentation style, fluent knowledge of photography, and the subject matter of place resonated deeply within me. At the end of the lecture, I bought her monograph and its pages turned me.

Even with their large scale, her photographs called to mind square snapshots. I remembered flipping through my father's photo albums he dubbed the ARCS (military lingo for archives) as the images told the stories of our lives. Kathleen's stunning work felt as intimate as a family photo album, but with the mysterious terrain of the Mississippi Delta. Her photographs offered compositions and images that sunk me into mud, alerted me to what might be darting overhead or clawing behind the skinning house. Her textures itched me. I had never witnessed photos that communicated to me in such deep and imagined ways. It was as if I was standing in the bean field or near where the Christmas deer hung. Through her photos of flatland and horizon, I came to see the size of my own life differently.

There is a vulnerability to the people in her photographs compared to the enormity of the world around them. I fret over her human subjects because the sky, the land, the horizon, the world is too imposing. It's nighttime outside Mr. Overstreet's trailer, and I say a prayer that he is safe inside with his family. Her book sweeps me into her familial landscape. It is as if I am scrolling through seasons and years, experiencing her family's farm, Belle Chase, as paint peels in the Victorian house built by her great-great-grandparents near fallow fields of shadows. Kathleen's past and present are offered to the viewer simultaneously. With each photograph I sense the movement and rustle of the Delta around me. The photographs place me in a lap of maternal rhythms. I enter a place haunting and alive with stories. Memories fall from these images as if they were a lock of her grandmother's hair or pressed flowers or a tattered commissary list.

There is the flapping and madness of disturbed birds on the margins of tree lines. There are footfalls and the sweat of weekly work in a canebrake world. I smell decay or wool socks soaked in a wetland drying near a fire by stuffed mallard ducks. I experience the plunging descent of brown winter on the Delta. Everything is captured on a continuum, alive or dead in a viewfinder. It is as if the teachings of her mother, grandmother, great grandmother, aunts, and cousins are rooted in ground. All the wisdom of kinswomen and their admonishments are captured in these images as if the arc of a woman's life by necessity grows slower, steadier, and higher than any man's. I enter Ryles chapel and hear rhythmic hymns and tongue-lashed sermons. I see foregrounds where Ben stood undaunted, and Asher goofed around outside a glass door obscured by the world's condensation. Blackbirds flock at dusk, darting and weaving. I feel my skin covered with mosquitoes.

Kathleen captures how large *place* is compared to us, how bitten we are by the past, how infected we become by time when we scratch too deep and why we can never escape its grave presence. But in the Delta, everything eventually flattens under the horizon's massiveness. She reminded me how baffling and perilous time, place, and memory are in our lives. Her book changed me

*

As a harbinger of what was to befall, in October of 2015, Hurricane Joaquin triggered 20 inches of rain over two days in Columbia. In the wake of devastation from burst dams and flash flooding, there was catastrophic damage to homes and businesses. Many were destroyed beyond repair. Many lives were forever altered.

Shortly after the rain finally stopped, I noticed cars pulling up to Kathleen's house and men and women dropping off boxes. Some folks entered the house holding what resembled hair dryers. Curious, I walked into the smell of a hundred wet dogs and saw Kathleen's dining room table transformed into a photographic restoration station. Volunteers were working around the table wetting the photos with clean water, delicately prying them apart, washing them, and patting and blowing them dry; and, if successful, lovingly wrapping them in tissue paper and tying them with ribbon.

They were rescuing photographs from houses inundated with floodwaters—photographs of weddings and Thanksgivings and Christmases and trips to beaches or to Italy. It was painstaking and heartbreaking work, as many times during the restoration process the emulsion tragically peeled across smiles, ruining the photos forever. Their efforts inspired me to write a poem titled, "Apertures" which appeared in *Marked by the Water: Artists Respond to a Thousand Year Flood*. This was not the last poem Kathleen would inspire me to write.

*

Although it seems like yesterday, on March 4, 2016, five months after Columbia's 1,000-year flood, my brother, the American novelist and memoirist Pat Conroy, died of pancreatic cancer. Six days later, I sent Kathleen a draft version of "Theology of Terrain," my ekphrasis poem inspired by her powerful photography and that of her friend Maude Schuyler Clay and by the clarity brought on by the loss of my brother. Whenever I would send Pat my poetry, he would encourage me with words like "You're on to something now," or "Dig deeper" or "You've shown a great leap." But I had never found the conviction to work through all the hours of mediocrity and failure until Pat's death. I found both conviction and voice—finally desperate and broken enough for me to claim them. With the Delta's immense space to free me, for the first time in my life I felt no occlusion of doubt. Kathleen's book *Into the Flatland* and her generous spirit changed my trajectory as a poet and writer.

A few months later she asked me to read my poem at the installation of her exhibit *Descent Mississippi Delta Photographs: 1999-2014* at the Columbia Museum of Art. It was an honor to read my poem at the installation next to her stunning photographs. Her husband, Ben and son, Asher beamed at her as she spoke to the crowd about her photographs in the exhibit.

*

On July 9, 2018, almost three years after the flood, Kathleen's husband, Ben Madden, age 49, left home for his early morning workout at the Drew Wellness Center to never return home to his family. Ben was a generous, dutiful, thoughtful, loving, and intuitive friend, husband, and father. He died from a swift cardiac event that seared profound grief into Kathleen's heart. Kathleen asked me to write a poem for the memorial service. Neither poetry nor photography can bring a husband or a brother or a sister or a mother or a grandmother back to us. Nor can they keep floodwaters from ruining a house or destroying photo albums or play with a nine-year-old son. They only give us a glimpse of the beauty and hardships of place, memory, and time. Our lives are as hard as loving each other and as difficult as unburdening sorrow to a world.

Since 2015, Kathleen has received acclaim for *Into the Flatland* and projects like "In Cotton." NPR's Claire O'Neill said of "In Cotton," "It's as much as photographic poem about memory, as it is a documentary project of what remains." Kathleen's photographs possess intimacy and immediacy but with the mysteries held in the margins between houses, churches, gravesites, fields, woods, ponds, and swamps. Her images live in places where decay and renewal trot across the landscape. Her photography invites us into fertile fields, incongruent from emotional detachment where we are drenched by rainstorms and sweat, blistered by time, and part of a proud bloodline. Kathleen's photographs and experiences remind us that life is a struggle, that places and time claim us, and that people show up to help. They teach us that to see beauty you must look for it and that a seed can be planted by a grandmother taping a message into a fertile book.

I open Kathleen's copy of *One Thousand Beautiful Things* and turn to a marked page to see in her grandmother's faded handwriting "my favorite author," with a lightly drawn arrow pointing to Archibald Rutledge's name under his essay, "I Got A Glory." I chuckle when I recall the story of my sixteen-year-old brother Pat's English teacher, Gene Norris, taking him to visit Rutledge at his Hampton Plantation near the Santee River because Pat dreamt of becoming a poet. It feels as if Rutledge wrote this for us:

> The only sure way out of suffering that I know is to find a glory, and to give to it the strength we might otherwise spend in despair.

I stare at the photographs in *Into the Flatland* and yell across imagined fields to Pam, Jessye, Bigma, Bama, Mary Carol and all the kinswomen from the Delta to tell them Kathleen found her glory in photography. They smile and holler back at me "Grief has always been as real and as big and as massive as the Delta's horizon." Her kinswomen, alive and dead, gaze at the same horizon and know—she takes glorious photographs despite it all. One never forgets the lessons of stubborn and enduring kinswomen.

*

To follow Professor Robbins' work, please visit her website: kathleen-robbins.com. Her work is currently on view at City Gallery in Charleston as part of Southbound curated by Mark Sloan and Mark Long.

SHARAN STRANGE
LOVE AND TERROR

By Len Lawson

> *I take the offerings of this slim life,*
> *hunger, like memory, some kind of assurance,*
> *the body, open, unable to be filled.*
>
> – *"Hunger," Sharan Strange*

Her given name and surname combined sound like a statement in the Southern, black vernacular: something a Carolina person might say to a friend about another. Although she reveals the surname's origin in one of her poems as "From a white man called Strange" (Line 11), by its definition, there may be something unfamiliar about a girl growing up in a rural Carolina town to conquer the hallowed halls of Harvard College and embark on a literary exodus leading to the impetus of an African American writers group known as the Dark Room Collective.

Something may be surprising about a Southern, black girl who escaped the clutches of poverty and racism to unleash a poet from her chest, breath, and lungs. A certain peculiarity may be derived from a brilliant mind trapped on dusty dirt roads held captive by systems of oppression made law. The slant alliteration of her name may have been a conjured spell to whisk the child away from everything she knew in 1960's and 1970's South Carolina, past the Appalachian Mountains of North Carolina and the Blue Ridge Mountains of Virginia north to an unfamiliar atmosphere to her.

As a young girl, she attempted to write a mystery novel inspired by her joy for reading. She became more inspired to write poetry due to correspondence between her older sister who wrote poetry and acclaimed poet Nikki Giovanni who encouraged Strange's sister.

Meeting black poets who shared her love for literature and blackness sparked within her what Audre Lorde called "the quality of light within which we predicate our hopes and dreams towards survival and change, first made into language, then into idea, then into more tangible action".

Sharan entered the world through Orangeburg, South Carolina, but became reborn in verse after visiting the funeral of James Baldwin with her housemate Thomas Sayers Ellis in 1987. The light within Sharan emerged after the two devised the Dark Room Collective, an organization promoting artists of color which launched the careers of poets such as former U.S. Poets Laureate Natasha Tretheway and Tracy K. Smith, The New Yorker poetry editor Kevin Young, Harvard Review poetry editor Major Jackson, and many more nationally well-known poets and writers. Being at the center of the Dark Room Collective allowed Strange to look back across those mountains and reflect upon her years in South Carolina with clarity, gravitas, and poise.

In 2000, Strange won the Barnard New Women Poets Prize for her manuscript *Ash*, selected by Sonia Sanchez who remarked that the collection is "economical in style, a subtle lyrical passion, that simmers even when the self barely survives. These poems resound with soldiering on this battlefield called life"

The book ranges from poetry on rural, Southern childhood and coming-of-age to reflections from various tales on black and Southern culture spotlighting people who could be from any South Carolina community before the turn of the century. Strange capitalizes on memory as a defining motif in the book with a close connection to family and heritage. She juxtaposes fondness for nature in the South with an exposé of systems that confine and manipulate one's potential tranquility amid the Southern landscape. She has commented on the irresolution of her feelings about the South recently: "I would say that my relationship to the South is one of ambivalence still at this point in my life. And I both love the South and...I sort of feel a great tension and in some ways a pushing away from that place."

Strange investigates themes of racism, alcoholism, rape, abuse, and miseducation all concentrated in the rural South. Although these are not exclusive to South Carolina, Strange had personal experience in the state throughout her formative years. She describes her experience in the state as "the abuse of the society as well as a sort of abuse in my home..." Her ambivalence remains and results in a concoction of these themes and more dubious trends in Southern life.

In the poem "Snow," Strange signifies school integration in the South with the nuance of a snow day in the South.

> The whites had finally stopped
> resisting. Unwanted at their school,
> we went anyway—historic, our parents
> intoned, eyes flashing caution
> to our measured breaths.

With this imagery, Strange conveys that integration in the South was as uncommon—if not as unwanted—as the falling snow. The Southern culture did not know how to integrate and what to do with these new conditions at first. To this day, there are still segregated public school events in the South. In the final stanza, Strange describes how they mixed the snow into ingredients for ice cream "that melted before we could savor it." The same can be said for school integration. Like the falling snow in the South, the nuance and celebration of integration would be short-lived. As Strange describes, the reality of integration like the snow became "...rude/ coldness, stinging, and wet..."

In 2013, Strange explained at a poetry reading for the Dark Room Collective 25th anniversary that the inscription for the poem is for Toi Derricotte, iconic co-founder of the Cave Canem black poetry collective, because at a poetry workshop facilitated by Derricotte participants were to write poems about a word given to them, and Strange's word was snow.

Her memory of this snow day as a child became infected with issues of race; separating her experiences in the South from racism remain virtually improbable. Strange's South Carolina mixes nature and trauma like the snow ice cream leaving a bitter taste with her that informs and saturates her poetry.

Strange addresses deficiencies in Southern education, especially in the context of race, with the poem "How to Teach Them." The four-part poem reveals windows into points of view from the Southern educator herself teaching generations of families yet ironically bearing no children of her own. "Her classroom was as orderly / as her childless home." Preparing for a school dance, the speaker depicts the boys' degrading selection process for girls in the class. "At school we learned...that our bodies could betray us...the boys chose eagerly // shunning the darker girls..." Even though the boys choose partners here based on skin color, the process is supervised by the teacher without correction; the only instruction given is to choose like enslaved people on an auction block. The most stunning imagery of the poem comes in the third part where the speaker's brother is struck by the teacher in discipline, causing his nose to bleed. The resolution remains even more unsettling. "We didn't consider charges, a lawsuit / but accepted the principal's astute / offer: a year of free lunch." In a humane and diplomatic culture, the teacher would have been suspended at the very least. The student victim's hunger becomes pacified as a means to assuage the violence upon the black boy, exhibiting a bitter microcosm of the justice system at large. Instead of going to trial, defendants are granted shorter sentences even if they committed no crime. Furthermore, the questionable justice of free lunch for a year does not address the issue that lunch must be paid for in public schools. In essence, the administration capitalizes here on the poverty of the black boy's family knowing their inability to make ends meet. The matter-of-fact tone of Strange's speaker unveils the casual manner in which incidents such as these occur in Southern education. She remarks that the nosebleed, "an instant protest," is the only resistance the boy has against the iron fist of white dominance in the South, the most permanent form of resistance being death.

In the poem "Froggy's Class" with the inscription South Carolina, 1969, another teacher emerges from Strange's South who must balance a classroom of white and black students. The educator's use of the term nigra for black people in the poem instantly denies her credibility Stuart Williams, a white student, uses the pronunciation "nee-gro" triumphantly in a speech in front of the class seen as a victory by the speaker who is the only black student in the class. She has to be concerned with her identity in this classroom before her education due to the racial slur emanating from the "gland-swollen throat" of the teacher. In what she refers to as her "first political memory", Strange recalls as a child hearing U.S. Senator Strom Thurmond (R-South Carolina) on the radio decisively and divisively state that for the life of his tenure African Americans would never be allowed to vote, shaping her view of not only politics and education in her birthplace but also her perception of self as marginalized before stepping outside her home or entering a classroom.

In a twist, Froggy drives the speaker home on the last day of school and gives her a notebook. A notebook could signify and foreshadow Strange's own beginnings as a writer and poet. Froggy's offering would be a tool toward the speaker practically continuing to make something of herself as Froggy tells her upon the speaker exits the car ; however, in the big picture, the speaker could use the notebook as a tool to pursue a writing career. Notwithstanding, she loathes accepting the gift from the teacher who has disrespected the speaker daily with racial slurs during the school year. Moreover, Strange reveals this imagery of the speaker reluctantly taking the notebook from Froggy almost as an afterthought since the speaker is more concerned with the teacher seeing her "squalid, small house." In his book Do You Know Enough about Me to Teach Me: A Student's Perspective, Dr. Stephen Peters, a former South Carolina public school administrator, highlights the principle of understanding minority students' points of view in education. The teacher must be cognizant of students' living environments and mindsets upon them entering the classroom. Although the speaker remains a stellar student among an all-white class, she stays preoccupied with adult situations and themes above her maturity level that immediately catapult her from her own childhood into the unforgiving, racist Southern education system. Strange, an eventual Harvard graduate, infuses her poetry with these types of memories not only exposing her former educators and inadequate Southern education system but also uncovering her ability to reflect and grow from such encounters as an adult, an educator in her own right at Spelman College, and as a poet from the depths of South Carolina's long history of racism and miseducation.

Strange also reveals childhood trauma in Ash stemming from her father's alcoholism. She has commented that this part of her childhood brings her terror to this day. Strange describes her father and her experiences living with him.

My father suffered from alcohol addiction…which ran in his family. He was also thwarted as an intelligent Black man who lived through Jim Crow, a man who, because of racism and poverty (and consequently little opportunity for education) was not able to live to his full potential, and who succumbed to alcoholism, the pathology of abuse, and the ravages of heart disease and diabetes that ended his life when he was 53. On his worst days, he took much of his pent-up frustrations and anger out on his family. On his better days, he was resourceful, creative, improvisational…and even though we were poor, he always took care of us materially, working whatever jobs he could despite his lack of education and white peoples' condescension. He kept a roof over our heads and food on the table. But he also wreaked emotional, psychological, and physical havoc in our lives—including his own. I never had a close relationship with him because I feared him (Personal Communication).

In "Grandmother's Clothes," Strange's speaker receives handmade clothes from her grandmother; nonetheless, this warm exchange takes a tragic turn when the speaker uncovers a flashback about her father stabbing her mother. She runs to her grandmother's arms for safety, and the grandmother in the poem declares a prophetic statement over the child: "Some things [Grandmother told me] I just won't hold on to" Referring to the dress, the grandmother also infers that the speaker will not always be inundated with these traumatic circumstances, and almost like a prayer, the grandmother's statement hopes better things for the speaker's future. Strange fled such memories when she left her native state to pursue her education. In the poem "Transits," Strange writes on more abuse of the father, stripping the child of the ability to dream.

> Once Father raised
> a broom to me—before
> possibility moved in me
> like blood, wouldn't flow, just
> backed up
> on itself, a sluggish creek—
> and raised a purple welt
> across my cheek

The stunning abuse causes the speaker to reflect on the end of childhood possibility and wonder before it can begin because of the harsh reality within the home. The psychological and emotional scars remain with the speaker as an adult, revealing at the end of the poem "Each month I still bleed, / feel the centrifugal / pull, refuse / my Father's house." The speaker cannot return to the place of pain for her which can be assumed is the Southern home she grew up in with an abusive father. The trauma of the beating lasts into her adulthood and becomes associated even with menstruation when blood breaches the body just as the speaker's blood breaches the surface of her face from the broom.

The subconscious effect of the abuse can be observed in the poem "Offering" where Strange writes about a recurring dream of the father. The speaker in the poem says in the dream she cooks rice for God and equates the tradition of throwing rice at weddings. The rice becomes "an offering that suggests [the bride's] first duty: to feed [the groom]." God and the groom here signify the father who in the second stanza appears in bed wrapped in "twisted sheets, a heavy mummy that will not eat or cry." The speaker in the dream lives to please her father "whom I never pleased" which becomes an impossible task, evidenced by the burned rice in the final stanza. Strange interprets the dream in her NPR appearance reading the poem.

I wrote the poem "Offering" upon waking up from a dream. And the poem deals with the complicated relationship that I had with my father and the imagery in the poem concerns the series of nightmares that I had following my father's death. In a way, I defied my father by leaving home early and striking out and seeking my own independence. Ultimately, I became something that my father never imagined me being, and that's an artist. So, I think of the poem as a tribute to the creative process. But I also feel that the poem was a step towards forgiving my father and healing that disconnection that we had.

Strange epitomizes overcoming the harsh conditions of the South to become someone greater than the circumstances of her humble beginnings. The poem is evidence that the father still haunts the psyche as with the speaker in "Transits," yet in reality the trauma propelled Strange to achieve her best self as a poet and scholar. "I saw leaving for college also as my getting away from both my father's chaos and the ugliness of the racist South."

Strange proves Audre Lorde's riveting words to be true about the power of poetry. "Our poems formulate the implications of ourselves, what we feel within, and dare make real...our fears, our hopes, our most cherished terrors." Concerning her feelings about her father today, Strange declares, "My relationship with him now is one of grief and forgiveness." Leaving this childhood abuse behind in South Carolina, she was able to compartmentalize, encapsulate, and harness these experiences into her poetry, suggesting that one must exit the South in order to be freed from it.

Strange illustrates the shame of childhood poverty further in her poem "Outhouses." Much like the speaker's shame in her small house at the end of "Froggy's Class," the speaker here describes the former outside restrooms in the South as "ignoble, embarrassing--/ a badge of / poverty..." However, the outhouses also bring the community together when they are built or removed. The "badges" worn by poor Southerners drew them closer together, a shadow of the famed Southern hospitality that the South boasts, yet in reality, it is only a veneer to disguise or distract the root of racism and classism which remains filthy and decayed as the unused outhouses in the poem or the excrement that they as foyers facilitate into the heart of the earth.

Strange's ambivalence toward the South his balanced by her feelings about the nature and reflective capabilities in the region. The verses of Southern poets bask in the imagery of fields, mountains, gardens, and wildlife. Strange's poetry clings to these markers of the South's identity as her verse strives to cover the trauma experienced in childhood.

What I do love about [the South] is the memories of nature: the sense of place, the sort of wildness and mysteries of that Southern rural landscape that I grew up in...and the joys of my encounters with the land as well as the sense of strength that I got from seeing my family, my community, eke out an existence in that place....the sense of begin cradled by nature.

Similar to the poem "Snow" where nature soothes the political upheaval taking place in the racial hotbed of South Carolina, Strange often uses imagery to alleviate the tension of intense themes in her poetry.

In the first poem of Ash, "Acts of Power" foreshadows the trauma of the book with the speaker nearly being hit by a car. She first encounters the innocence of nature with friends before the shocking event.

> I sat
> in a field among tall green reeds whose
> cayenne-colored tips waved like anemones.
> We'd suck the salty juices from the stalks.
> Taste of our thirsty bodies, taste of
> The source of life, the sea

The speaker delights in the intoxicating nature of the reeds and the pure, juvenile bliss that nature exudes until she is swept back into the dangers of reality signified by the oncoming vehicle she apparently does not see. The scenario presents a microcosm of Strange's perception of the South in her childhood. The tragedy in the truth of Southern life brought on by humanity beyond hospitality and community upsets one's ability to appreciate the beauty of nature. Children become thrust into adult situations and themes before they have matured to understand their function in the dystopian Southern society. Strange sets up further dangers to childhood with the abrupt shift from love to terror in this poem.

In the poem "Childhood," Strange exhibits a more utopian view of Southern life as children catch fireflies in the summer. The fireflies signify the children themselves. "They lit our evenings like dreams / we thought we couldn't have" (Strange Lines 2-3). Here in the first stanza, the speaker describes the fireflies as unattainable beacons of light beyond their capture. In the subsequent stanzas, the children embrace the fireflies' abilities to illuminate the skies and the children's possibilities to become more than their environment can provide. "They gave us new faith / in the nasty tonics of childhood...and we silently vowed to swallow ever after." Despite the process of adolescence and puberty, the children believe in themselves through the luminescence of the fireflies in front of their eyes. They too can become lights of the world. "We wanted their brilliance / small fires hovering-- / each tiny explosion / the birth of a new world." The idea of escape from the "tonics" of reality in the South that would keep them grounded lifts the children into dreams above their present hardships and realities. Nature here serves as a catalyst for interrupting the narratives of poverty and abuse that riddle families in the South. Strange has remarked about her poem that the fireflies represent "mystery and a sense of possibility...something greater beyond myself... a sense of something that I can be, something larger than what I was." Strange reminds readers of the power in nature's wildness to transform people from being entrenched or even buried by the surrounding circumstance of Southern life.

A comparable escape from reality into nature can be detected in the poem "Jimmy's First Cigarette" in which the title subject inhales and leaves the present moment for a brief getaway "numbing [Jimmy] to the possibility // of pain and cruelty in the world." Strange illustrates how even a toxic narcotic such as a cigarette can provide temporary relief from Southern life.

> From your Grandma's porch
> you surveyed a lush green countryside
> murmuring with the traffic
>
> of laughing birds and wild animals
> and ghosts...

Strange's wildness in nature emerges here with the possibilities of discovering the mysteries in nature, even the supernatural.
In "Jimmy's," the setting is the countryside of Orangeburg County, South Carolina, my grandmother's place in the backwoods. I

remember the air always feeling "thick" there, having this weight and presence. It seemed to me that I could feel history in that place, the history of family and of the South. It was a marvelous thing to me. And that "thickness," that pregnant quality to the air, that was the "traffic of ghosts."

Natives of South Carolina, especially African Americans, often speak of the supernatural in the form of folklore such as ghosts, hags, voodoo, or roots. These allusions also appear in the poems "The Crazy Girl," "Miz Mattie," and "The Stranger." As with the reeds in the poem "Childhood," another natural herb here catapults Jimmy into a realm that shields him from dealing with adult situations. In an interview with Toi Dericotte for Callaloo, Strange acknowledges this escape. "The main issue is how this child, and by extension, children in general, can be exposed to harsh, and often painful lessons, emotionally as well as physically. It's about loss of innocence—and for male children this can indeed be harsh" ("An Interview"). However, also similar to "Childhood," Jimmy's escape remains short-lived when "…daddy's belt broke / your childish reverie…," ushering Jimmy's "abrupt trip back to reality." Strange comments on this trip from "reverie" to discipline by Jimmy's elders who are supposed to protect him rather than abuse him.

The poem deals with the arbitrary cruelness adults commit in teaching children certain lessons. And how, paradoxically, it is often the ones whom the children are entrusted to, whom they trust and look to for love, kindness, sustenance, nurturance, protection, and those kinds of things—you know, parents, family. I don't believe my father and grandmother deliberately planned to teach my brother that particular lesson in that particular fashion but acted possibly spontaneously to punish him for overstepping his bounds—although he was acting out of a natural curiosity, and a desire to act out a fantasy of being a man by imitating his father.

Strange here discusses another reality to children in the South which is corporal punishment as a form of discipline that often crosses the border of abuse. As also vividly illustrated in the poem "Transits," the generational practice of parental corporal punishment can thwart children's ability to perceive nature's and their own possibilities although in this sense the elders seek to prevent Jimmy from harming himself. Strange wonders, "Or maybe they were reenacting some draconian rite of passage from their past. I don't know. Nothing was explained." Explanation or understanding usually didn't or doesn't accompany parental corporal punishment; children are left to understand mostly for themselves the harshness of the physicality. Ironically, the elders do more harm to him psychologically by striking him than the cigarette can do to him physically just as the oncoming car hurtles the speaker back into reality by force in "Childhood."

Despite feelings of ambivalence towards South Carolina, Strange still visits her relatives although both her parents are deceased. Along with memories shared with family and friends, some of her fondest memories are of the South Carolina Lowcountry such as St. Helena Island, a central location for the Gullah/Geechie nation, giving her a strong sense of ancestry and history.

Strange has also become more invested in the poetry community in South Carolina. In 2017, she served as keynote speaker for an annual poetry workshop held by The Watering Hole, an organization founded in South Carolina for poets of color. As co-founder of the groundbreaking Dark Room Collective, Strange advocates for community in poetry, especially among artists of color. The journey of Sharan Strange, therefore, exemplifies the quest for possibility despite one's upbringing. She considers her decision to leave South Carolina and its reverberations in her life to date as crucial. Had she not left South Carolina, she may have never realized that possibility of growing her poetry craft, developing her own voice through verse, or admiring other writers to the extent of creating the Dark Room Collective to celebrate them and facilitate other voices like her own. Her views on disengaging from the Palmetto State, however, provide more balance to this theory.

... each person's experience is unique...ultimately, in terms of influence, I think the integrity, significance, and compelling nature of the poet's voice and work would matter most...[The South] still lacks some of those resources of traditional bastions of literary establishment that can determine whose work becomes known and how universally (for example, major presses, writing programs, fellowships, prizes/awards). Certainly, we have a (somewhat) more democratized landscape with the pervasiveness and innovations of digital technology and more institutional footholds, but old attitudes, power dynamics, and centers of influence still hold sway in many ways... Saint Gwendolyn [Brooks] (as I like to call her, after seeing that haloed portrait of her on the cover of the June 2017 issue of Poetry) said, "Art urges voyages..." My sense is that we South Carolina poets, like other artists, are simply compelled to follow that urge, a drive for discovery...whether it takes us out of the state or not.

Whether the journey is deemed as escape, flight, hunger, or voyage, movement appears to be a trend among South Carolina poets of color, and why would it not be, considering how African ancestors entered America? Movement has always been in black persons' bones whether escaping from cruel masters or toward unprecedented opportunity and possibility. There is nothing strange about that, but for James Sr.'s daughter Sharan, migration to the North provides harrowing insight through verse into what it means to be black, female, and Southern in Carolina.

KAY THIGPEN
POWERING THE MAGIC

By Chad Henderson

Kay Thigpen doesn't suffer fools, nor does she tolerate foolishness. Yes, I refuse to use the past tense when writing about this woman who changed a community's entertainment values, impacted countless theatre artists nationwide, and loved her family (blood and chosen) with intense loyalty and support. Her influence and impact are ongoing. Just ask anyone who spent a little time at Trustus Theatre – the brainchild of Kay and her late husband, Jim, who died in 2017. She's always going to be with us.

Kay and Jim started Trustus Theatre in 1985. Kay was the managing director and Jim was the artistic director before they retired, (forgive the past tense). With an empty nest, a second mortgage, and a desire to bring cutting edge theatre to Columbia, they created the professional contemporary theatre that now lives at the base of the Vista district. In its 37th Season now, Trustus won the SC Governor's Award for the Arts in 2000 and the SC Theatre Association's Theatre of Distinction Award in 2014.

But back to my original point: fools and foolishness.

Kay "went home" (she'd hate that) on September 20, 2021. She knew it was coming. She had cancer and it was terminal. She wasn't going to go through endless bouts of treatment because she'd "lived a full life, and it is what it is." This is what she said when she called to tell me the news. Fighting the inevitable would have been "foolishness," which Kay would never be a party to. So, with the same matter-of-fact approach she'd used the entire time I'd known her she accepted that her clock was ticking.

When I say Kay doesn't suffer fools or tolerate foolishness, it doesn't mean she doesn't know how to let loose and have a good time. "Let's check props" means *I'll roll a number and smoke it in the shop with you.* "We're going to the beach" means *the family is going to the coast this summer, don't bother me or burn anything down.* "Good job, honey" means *you may have possibly just done your best work yet.*

(AN ASIDE) *PRO TIPS FOR WORKING UNDER KAY'S MANAGEMENT:* Don't ask for more money in a production budget. If you ask for more money, you better be damn sure that purchase is going to serve the theatre for longer than one show. Don't be an asshole as a customer – if you do that too much, she'll tell you to never come back. Smoking in non-public spaces (like offices) is not against the law as she interprets it. The actors have to project – she can't hear them. The music in the show is TOO LOUD. Friday is for Jin Jin's Chinese takeout before the show. She will sweep the entryway of the theatre with that same old broom that hides in the back of the bar – don't offer to do it for her, that's her thing. Jim is going to buy that damn jar of Gefilte fish on Jewish holidays, but don't take it when he offers it, it's blech, she says. Max, her grandson, is everything to her.

The greatest testament to her management style is her *grace*. Always grace. When she sees people being imperfect human beings, she gives them the allowance to learn from their mistakes and become stronger, a management style that many leaders and governing boards could learn from. She believes that as long as the work gets done, then there's no need to satisfy every working minute of a 40-hour work week prescribed by an establishment she's not a part of. And let people work when they're productive, damn it! Strange, I've heard this same philosophy at countless theatre conferences recently. Guess she's ahead of her time (no surprise there).

I tried to avoid the past tense in writing this remembrance because the lessons this woman instilled in me will live there forever. She's here with us every day. As the lights shine on the marquees outside of Trustus Theatre, Kay and Jim are the power making that magic happen. It's like the kids standing outside of Willy Wonka's factory: something is going on in that building. Something that started 37 years ago with boldness, confidence, and a belief in this city. They expected more of Columbia artists and audiences, and they gave it to us – whether we knew we needed it or not. It's funny, a risk like they took might seem foolish to some people, but I guess they knew something we didn't.

Kay don't worry about us – we'll sweep the entryway. We'll banish fools and foolishness (as much as we can). And yes, we'll kindly decline the Gefilte fish.

But we will never forget everything you taught us, and we will love you forever.

A version of the above previously appeared in *Jasper Magazine, Fall 2021*.

About the Contributors

David Axe is a writer and filmmaker in Columbia, South Carolina.

Retired English instructor **Dale A. Bailes** commutes from the 'hood in Pawleys to the 'wood in Columbia for his part-time work as a Standardized Patient at the U of SC School of Nursing. His poems have been published in *Fall Lines* and *American Writers Review*.

Claudia Smith Brinson worked as a journalist at newspapers in Greece, Florida, and South Carolina for more than 30 years. She spent the majority of her journalism career with Knight Ridder at *The State* newspaper, working as a senior writer, national writing coach, columnist, and associate editor for the editorial page. In 2006, she joined Columbia College in Columbia, SC, directing the Writing for Print and Digital Media major and an internship program, and holding the Harriet Gray Blackwell endowed professorship. She won more than three dozen awards for her journalism, was the first person to win Knight Ridder's Award of Excellence twice and was a member of *The State* team whose work on Hurricane Hugo was a Pulitzer finalist. She has published essays in women's magazines, and her short fiction awards include the O. Henry. In 2020, the University of South Carolina Press published her book *Stories of Struggle: The Clash Over Civil Rights in South Carolina*. She is working with civil rights photographer Cecil J. Williams on a 2023 book that will include her text on the SC civil rights movement in the 1940s, '50s, and '60s and eighty of Williams's photos.

Cindi Boiter is a six-time winner of the SC Fiction Project, winner of the Piccolo Fiction Project, the Porter Fleming Award for fiction, the 2014 recipient of the Elizabeth O'Neill Verner Governor's Award for the Arts, and the 2018 recipient of the Lucy Hampton

Bostick Award for literary advocacy. She is the founder and editor of *Jasper Magazine*, *The Limelight* volumes I, II, and III, *A Sense of the Midlands*, *Art from the Ashes*, *Marked by the Water*, *Setting the Supper Table*, *Sheltered*, and editor and founder of the literary magazine *Fall Lines – a literary convergence*, author of *Buttered Biscuits—Short Stories from the South*, and literary author of *Red Social*. Cindi is the executive director of The Jasper Project and is married to Dr. Bob Jolley, with whom she founded Muddy Ford Press in 2011.

Tim Conroy is a poet and former educator. His work has appeared in *Fall Lines*, *Blue Mountain Review*, *Jasper*, *Marked by the Water*, *Sheltered*, *Twelve Mile Review*, *The Post and Courier*, *Ukweli: Searching for Healing Truth*, and *Our Prince of Scribes: Writers Remember Pat Conroy*. In 2017, Muddy Ford Press published Tim's book of poetry, *Theologies of Terrain*, edited by Ed Madden. A founding board member of the Pat Conroy Literary Center established in his brother's honor, Tim and his wife Terrye live in Dunedin, Florida.

Clair DeLune has worked as a journalist, syndicated columnist, media relations professional, editor, photographer, artist, producer, and historian. She taught music history courses as well as journalism writing at the University of South Carolina and hosted *Blues Moon Radio* for 29 years. Presently, she works as a writer, PR practitioner and digital strategist. She is a contributing author to *Making Notes: Music of the Carolinas* from Novello Festival Press; *State of the Heart: SC authors on the places they love* from USC Press; and *Limelight II* from Muddy Ford Press. She is the author of the bestselling book, *South Carolina Blues*, a pictorial history of 500 years of roots music in our state, published by Arcadia Press.

A former journalist, **Kristine Hartvigsen** works in marketing at Piedmont Technical College. Her writing has appeared in *Jasper, Columbia Metropolitan, Lake Murray, Columbia Living, Columbia/Charleston/Greenville Business Monthly, SC Business*, and

Sandlapper magazines as well as literary collections that include *Fall Lines: A Literary Convergence*, *The Limelight*, and *State of the Heart*. Muddy Ford Press published her first poetry collection, *To the Wren Nesting*, in 2012. She has a new collection coming out — *The Soul Mate Poems* — which will be published in 2023 by Finishing Line Press.

Chad Henderson served as company member, marketing director, artistic director, and executive director of Trustus Theatre over the course of 14 years. He's currently a freelance director and the marketing and communications director at the SC Philharmonic. In the 2022-23 season he is directing *Clyde's, Don't Let the Pigeon Drive the Bus*, and *Hundred Days*. He recently directed the staged reading of *Moon Swallower* by Colby Quick for the Jasper Project's Play Right Series.

Len Lawson is author of Negro Asylum for the Lunatic Insane (Main Street Rag, 2023), *Chime* (Get Fresh Books, 2019), and the chapbook *Before the Night Wakes You* (Finishing Line Press, 2017). He is also co-editor of *The Future of Black: Afrofuturism, Black Comics, and Superhero Poetry* (Blair Press, 2021) and co-author of *Hand in Hand: Poets Respond to Race* (Muddy Ford Press, 2017). South Carolina Humanities awarded him a 2022 Governors Award for Fresh Voices in the Humanities. He has received fellowships from Tin House, Palm Beach Poetry Festival, Callaloo Barbados, Vermont Studio Center, and Virginia Center for the Creative Arts among others. His poetry appears in *African American Review, Callaloo, Mississippi Review, Ninth Letter, Verse Daily, Poetry Northwest*, and has been translated internationally. Len earned a Ph.D. in English Literature and Criticism at Indiana University of Pennsylvania. A South Carolina native, he is currently Assistant Professor of English at Newberry College.

Ed Madden is the author of four books of poetry. A fifth, *A Pooka in Arkansas*, was selected for the 2022 Hilary Tham Prize and will be published by The Word Works in 2023. His work has been published in *American Poets, Crazyhorse, Image, Poetry Ireland Review, Prairie Schooner, storySouth*, and other journals, as well as in *The Forward Book of Poetry*, He is a professor of English and the former director of Women's and Gender Studies at the University of South Carolina, where he teaches Irish literature, queer studies, and creative writing. From 2015 through 2022, Madden served as the poet laureate for the City of Columbia, SC. He is recipient of an Academy of American Poets Laureate Fellowship and a 2019 artist's residency at the Instituto Sacatar in Itaparica, Brazil.

Cassie Premo Steele, is an award-winning ecofeminist author of 16 books. Her novel, *The ReSisters*, published by a small, independent press in Maine, was a #1 bestseller on Amazon in the category of books for young people combating prejudice and racism. *We Heal from Memory*, her scholarly work published by Palgrave, advanced ideas about the power of poetry to heal individual and collective trauma twenty years before these ideas were introduced into the mainstream. Her nonfiction book, *Earth Joy Writing*, published by Ashland Creek Publishing in Oregon, continues to sell well seven years after publication and is available for sale at Congaree National Park, where she leads seasonal forest journaling workshops. Her poetry has won numerous awards, including the Archibald Rutledge Prize named after the first Poet Laureate of SC, where she lives with her wife.

Jason Stokes is a 1999 graduate of USC with an emphasis in film and a film studies minor. His film and television work includes *The Patriot, Necessary Roughness, Banshee,* and *Shots Fired*. His theatre work includes *Rent, The Rocky Horror Show, Streetcar, Cat on a Hot Tin Roof, The Full Monty,* and *A Funny Thing Happened on the Way to the Forum*. His play *Composure* premiered in August 2022 at Trustus Theatre.

Jon Tuttle is Director of University Honors and professor of English at Francis Marion University. His plays, which include The *Hammerstone, Drift, Holy Ghost, The Sweet Abyss, The Palace of* *the Moorish Kings, and Boy About Ten*, have been produced at Trustus Theatre and theatres across the country and published in *The Trustus Collection* (Muddy Ford Press). His next book, *South Carolina Onstage,* will be published by Academica Press in September. He is a recipient of the South Carolina Governor's Award in the Humanities.

Joshua Tuttle is a musician and educator based in Cincinnati, OH. He holds degrees from the University of South Carolina (BM), Bowling Green State University (MM), and is currently completing his Doctorate of Musical Arts at the University of Cincinnati College-Conservatory of Music. As a researcher and advocate, much of his focus is on promoting contemporary classical music by living composers. Most recently, he has performed at the Bowling Green New Music festival, the US Navy Band Symposium, and the North American Saxophone Alliance (NASA) Biennial Conference, and has collaborated with celebrated composers Stacy Garrop, Marilyn Shrude, and John Fitz Rogers.

Cover Artist

The cover art was created intentionally for this book by Columbia, SC-based artist Michael Krajewski. His style has been described as neo-expressionist, but he's less concerned with labeling than with creating from an authentic, mindful space and expressing what he's feeling and experiencing in the moment. He works in mixed media and has experimented with everything from multimedia integrations to painting on live models. His work has been featured in numerous galleries in South Carolina, including Anastasia & Friends, Grapes & Gallery, HofP Gallery, Frame of Mind, The City Gallery at Waterfront Park - Charleston, and Tapp's Art Center. He's been commissioned to provide artwork for film and art festivals, set design for Trustus Theatre, and art for the Columbia City Ballet. Michael has painted a mural in the Greenville Children's Museum, which was sponsored by Target Corporation, and a mural in the Columbia Museum of Art, where he remains one of only two artists ever invited to paint on the walls. His most recent art installation is an ongoing massive canvas created from the walls of the restaurant The Black Rooster in West Columbia, SC, where the artist continues to install his paintings directly on the walls of the entire restaurant space. Michael is represented by HoFP Gallery.

www.ingramcontent.com/pod-product-compliance
Lightning Source LLC
Chambersburg PA
CBHW041129110526
44592CB00020B/2739